# Daily
# Whispers
## OF
# Faith

*365 Devotional Thoughts for Women*

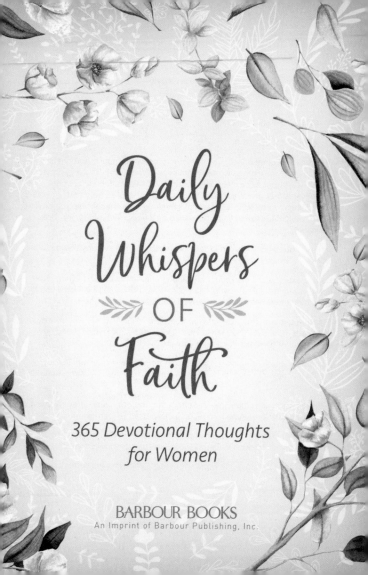

# Daily Whispers OF Faith

## 365 Devotional Thoughts for Women

BARBOUR BOOKS

An Imprint of Barbour Publishing, Inc.

Member of the
Evangelical Christian
Publishers Association

Printed in China.

# Introduction

Like the deep roots of a plant drawing support and nourishment from the ground, your faith in God provides an anchorage for the rest of your life. You can't have true peace, joy, and purpose without surrendering to and trusting in your heavenly Father's care. He will uphold and nourish you. *Daily Whispers of Faith* offers a year's worth of inspiration as you draw nearer to God in faith—strengthened and blossoming each day.

*Plant your roots in Christ and let him be the foundation for your life.*
COLOSSIANS 2:7 CEV

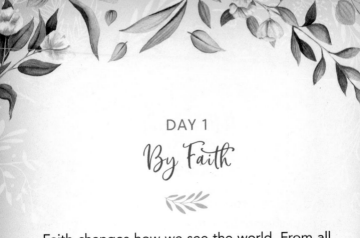

## DAY 1

# By Faith

Faith changes how we see the world. From all appearances, your circumstances may seem daunting. Your opportunities limited. Your future set in stone. But when you place your faith in God instead of what you see, your heart can't help but overflow with hope. God's power is at work behind the scenes. He's working in both you and your circumstances. He promises to bring something good out of every situation, no matter how things may look on the outside. Today, "live by faith, not by sight" (2 Corinthians 5:7 NIV).

## DAY 2
### Father God

"See what great love the Father has lavished on us, that we should be called children of God! And that is what we are!" (1 John 3:1 NIV). God's Word declares His love for us—He is almighty God, yet He loves us as His children. He "lavishes" His love on us. What an amazing thought! When your faith wanes, think on the vastness of God's love. He will sustain you as only a loving Father can.

## DAY 3
# Faith's Proof

*Do we love God? Do we keep his commands? The proof that we love God comes when we keep his commandments and they are not at all troublesome. Every God-begotten person conquers the world's ways. The conquering power that brings the world to its knees is our faith. The person who wins out over the world's ways is simply the one who believes Jesus is the Son of God.*

1 JOHN 5:3–5 MSG

## DAY 4

## A Provision of Faith

When we talk about provision, our physical needs first come to mind: food, water, shelter, and the like. But we have spiritual needs that are just as essential as the air we breathe. We thirst for God's forgiveness and hunger for His love. Those who haven't yet put their faith in God often try filling this need with power, possessions, or relationships. But only a relationship with God can fill this void. Only faith provides wholeness to a broken world.

## DAY 5

# Total Healing to Come

When you reach out in faith, God starts the process of healing old wounds. But there are some wounds that won't completely heal this side of heaven. Like a former injury that aches with an approaching storm, past emotional scars may ache at unexpected times. Scars are signs of healing, a step toward wholeness. Thank God for the healing He's brought your way. But, when Jesus returns, He'll wipe away every tear. That's when you'll truly be healed and whole.

## DAY 6

### An Unlikely Pair

"Trouble" and "joy" may seem an unlikely pair, something akin to sardines and chocolate syrup. But God seems to prefer the unlikely. He chose a speech-impaired Moses as His spokesman and simple fishermen as missionaries. These choices brought challenges. But when faith is pushed to its limits, God works in wonderfully unlikely ways. Regard troubles as opportunities instead of obstacles. As you rely on God, His glory will shine through you—and unexpected joy will be your reward.

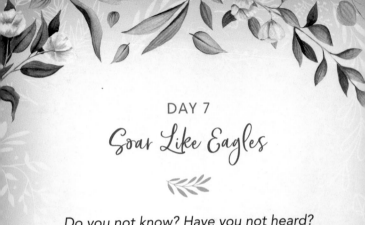

## DAY 7

# *Soar Like Eagles*

Do you not know? Have you not heard?
The Lᴏʀᴅ is the everlasting God, the Creator
of the ends of the earth. He will not grow
tired or weary, and his understanding no one
can fathom. He gives strength to the weary
and increases the power of the weak. Even
youths grow tired and weary, and young men
stumble and fall; but those who hope in the
Lᴏʀᴅ will renew their strength. They will soar
on wings like eagles; they will run and not
grow weary, they will walk and not be faint.

Isᴀɪᴀʜ 40:28–31 ɴɪᴠ

## DAY 8

### Beyond Senses

Faith does not mean believing without evidence. It means believing in realities that go beyond sense and sight—for which a totally different sort of evidence is required.

JOHN BAILLIE

Sight is not faith and hearing is not faith, neither is feeling faith; but believing when we neither see, hear, nor feel is faith; and everywhere the Bible tells us our salvation is to be by faith. Therefore we must believe before we feel, and often against our feelings, if we would honor God by our faith.

HANNAH WHITALL SMITH

## DAY 9

### Friends Matter

Jesus' disciples were more than just apprentices learning the ins and outs of faith. They were also Jesus' closest friends. They walked together, talked together, ate together, and prayed together. When Jesus knew His time on earth was short, He turned to them for support. Follow Jesus' example. No matter how busy you get, make time for the friends God brings into your life. They may be God's answers to prayers you're praying today.

# Nothing More, Nothing Less

God created you to live forever with Him. But like every other person since the dawn of time, you turned away from God to live life on your own terms. Yet God didn't give up on you. He sent His Son to pay the heavy price of your rebellion, to sacrifice His life for yours. When you place your faith in Jesus, you accept this gift. Your salvation's complete. There's nothing more, or less, you can do to be saved.

## DAY 11
### Faith for the Future

For centuries, people have turned to fortunetellers, crystal balls, and horoscopes in the hope of glimpsing the future. Turning to anything, or anyone, other than God for this kind of information is futile, as well as forbidden by scripture. It's also unnecessary. God holds our future in His hands. He has a plan and a purpose for what lies ahead. We may not know the details of all our tomorrows, but faith assures us it's well worth waiting for.

# DAY 12

## Reassuring Presence

GOD, investigate my life; get all the
facts firsthand. I'm an open book to you;
even from a distance, you know what I'm
thinking. You know when I leave and when
I get back; I'm never out of your sight.
You know everything I'm going to say before
I start the first sentence. I look behind me
and you're there, then up ahead and you're
there, too—your reassuring presence,
coming and going. This is too much,
too wonderful—I can't take it all in!

PSALM 139:1–6 MSG

# Control Yourself!

Self-control is attractive, to others and to God. That's because self-control reflects God's own character. God doesn't act on a whim. He waits for just the right time to do just the right thing. Is there any area of your life where you wish you had more self-control? God can help. Perhaps you need to lose weight, just say no to gossip, or keep your temper in check. Ask God for the desire, and the discipline, to wisely exercise restraint. And have faith that He will follow through.

## DAY 14

## Even Seas

*And, behold, there arose a great tempest in the sea, insomuch that the ship was covered with the waves: but he was asleep. And his disciples came to him, and awoke him, saying, Lord, save us: we perish. And he saith unto them, Why are ye fearful, O ye of little faith? Then he arose, and rebuked the winds and the sea; and there was a great calm. But the men marvelled, saying, What manner of man is this, that even the winds and the sea obey him!*

MATTHEW 8:24–27 KJV

## DAY 15

# Faithfully Devoted

Thank You for living water. You are the Holy
One of my life. As You run an entire universe,
I wonder how You can be concerned with me,
but Your Word speaks of Your faithfulness to
even the humblest of Your children. I praise
You, O Lord, that You consider me a treasure
and that You love me with Your unconditional
and everlasting love. Make me a woman
who is faithfully devoted to You. Amen.

# DAY 16
## A Fruitful Life

Do you ever feel like you're running in circles—that your life has little purpose or that you're not being as fruitful for the Lord as you'd like to be? No matter what your circumstances are, God has a plan for you, and that plan is not out of reach. Have faith in our all-powerful God! As long as you are looking to Him, your life will be fruitful and fulfilling. That's His will, His promise, His plan.

## Close to Him

The enormous wealth of love God has for you compels Him to shower you with His presence. The fresh scent that remains after a spring rain shower is an open invitation to rest in His mercy and grace. The flutter of a hummingbird's wings or the gentle sigh from a toddler's crib sends a special message that expresses His desire to satisfy your heart with everything good. Allow your faith to draw you close to Him.

## *On Your Side*

[Jesus said,] "You are those who have stood by me in my trials. And I confer on you a kingdom, just as my Father conferred one on me, so that you may eat and drink at my table in my kingdom and sit on thrones, judging the twelve tribes of Israel. Simon, Simon, Satan has asked to sift all of you as wheat. But I have prayed for you, Simon, that your faith may not fail. And when you have turned back, strengthen your brothers."

LUKE 22:28–32 NIV

DAY 19

## In Every Circumstance

The light and life of God lives in you, therefore the blessing of truth is always available to you, helping you know and discern what is good and right for your life. Jesus never promised your pathway would be easy, but He has promised to never leave you. Truth is always with you. And you can call upon Him in every circumstance to light your way. Trust Him to keep His promise. Have faith in His guiding light.

## DAY 20

# Rich in Faith

Being rich in faith is the secret to leading an abundant life. That's because faith allows us to see life from God's perspective. We begin to appreciate how much we have instead of focusing on what we think we lack. We understand that what's of eternal worth is more valuable than our net worth. We feel rich, regardless of how much, or how little, we own. True abundance flows from the inside out, from God's hand straight to our hearts.

# DAY 21

## Clothe Your Heart

For many women, getting dressed is a bit like painting a portrait. They put themselves together in a way that reflects how they want others to see them. Successful? Confident? Youthful? A bit of a rebel? Who you are within speaks much louder than what you wear on the outside. As you allow God, through faith, to clothe your heart in love and compassion, you'll automatically become more attractive. You'll draw others toward you and God, regardless of what you have on.

### DAY 22

## Mutual Encouragement

*I long to see you so that I may impart to you some spiritual gift to make you strong— that is, that you and I may be mutually encouraged by each other's faith. I do not want you to be unaware, brothers and sisters, that I planned many times to come to you (but have been prevented from doing so until now) in order that I might have a harvest among you, just as I have had among the other Gentiles.*

ROMANS 1:11–13 NIV

# DAY 23

## Sure Faith

Faith, in and of itself, is nothing more than trust. If you place your trust in something that isn't trustworthy, your faith is futile. You can have faith that money grows on trees, but ultimately that faith isn't going to help you pay your bills. Putting your faith in Jesus is different. Historical and biblical eyewitness accounts back up Jesus' claims. That means putting your faith in Jesus is both logical and powerful. It's a faith that won't fail.

DAY 24

## Faith That Moves

If we desire to praise God more, we must ask for grace that our private devotions may rise to a higher standard. A living faith is not something you have to carry, but something that carries you.

J. H. OLDHAM

A true faith in Jesus Christ will not suffer us to be idle. No, it is an active, lively, restless principle; it fills the heart, so that it cannot be easy till it is doing something for Jesus Christ.

GEORGE WHITEFIELD

## Blessings Everywhere

Blessings are gifts straight from God's hand. Some of them are tangible, like the gift of a chance acquaintance leading to a job offer that winds up helping to pay the bills. Some are less concrete. They may come wrapped in things like faith, joy, clarity, and contentment appearing seemingly out of "nowhere" amid difficult circumstances. The more frequently you thank God for His blessings, the more aware you'll be of how many more there are to thank Him for.

### DAY 26

# No Bragging

And God gave Jesus to show today that he
does what is right. God did this so he could
judge rightly and so he could make right
any person who has faith in Jesus. So do we
have a reason to brag about ourselves? No!
And why not? It is the way of faith that stops
all bragging, not the way of trying to obey
the law. A person is made right with God
through faith, not through obeying the law.

ROMANS 3:26–28 NCV

# DAY 27
## Faith Workout

People joke about how women sit around eating bonbons all day. You know firsthand that nothing is further from the truth. You face challenges each and every day. Instead of viewing challenges as negative, faith helps you see them as opportunities for growth. In the same way that strengthening your body is difficult and often uncomfortable, strengthening your faith can be the same way. But the outcome is worth the challenge. A stronger faith results in a more balanced life.

## DAY 28

*At Ease*

No mother's child is "ordinary." Love enables parents to see their children's unique gifts and potential—and instills in them the desire to protect their children at any cost. Your heavenly Father feels the same way about you and your children. When fear for your children's health or happiness threatens your peace of mind, let faith put your mind at ease. God cares for your children in ways that reach far beyond your own abilities.

# DAY 29

## Because of Hope

We have heard about the faith you have in
Christ Jesus and the love you have for all
of God's people. You have this faith and
love because of your hope, and what you
hope for is kept safe for you in heaven.
You learned about this hope when you
heard the message about the truth,
the Good News that was told to you.
Everywhere in the world that Good
News is bringing blessings
and is growing.

Colossians 1:4–6 ncv

## DAY 30

### Crystal Clear

*Thank You, Lord, that Your truth is not a mystery. I don't have to wonder if I've lived a good enough life to reach heaven. I don't have to search the world over to discover Your wisdom. All I have to do is accept Your gracious gift of salvation and reach out to Your Word. Your truth is readily available, Lord. I know with certainty that I will one day see You face-to-face. Deepen my faith so that I might penetrate the spiritual darkness around me. Amen.*

# DAY 31
## Amazing Results

In the Bible, God asked people to do some pretty unlikely things. Build an ark. Defeat Jericho by walking around its walls. Battle a giant with a slingshot. But when people are committed to doing what God asks, amazing things happen. What's God asking you to do? Love someone who seems unlovable? Break a bad habit? Forgive? Commit yourself to follow through and do what God asks. Through faith, you'll witness firsthand how the unbelievable can happen.

## DAY 32
### Faith Like Children

*Some people brought their little children to Jesus so he could touch them, but his followers told them to stop. When Jesus saw this, he was upset and said to them, "Let the little children come to me. Don't stop them, because the kingdom of God belongs to people who are like these children. I tell you the truth, you must accept the kingdom of God as if you were a little child, or you will never enter it."*

MARK 10:13–15 NCV

## DAY 33
### God-Confidence

You're a beautiful, gifted woman. God created you that way. You have countless reasons to be confident in what you do, who you are, and where you're headed—but those reasons don't rest on your talents, intelligence, accomplishments, net worth, or good looks. They rest solely on God and His faithfulness. Living a life of faith means trading self-confidence for God-confidence. It means holding your head high because you know you're loved and that God's Spirit is working through you.

## DAY 34

*Step out in Faith*

Why do you need courage today? To apologize? To forgive? To break an old habit? To discipline a child? To love in the face of rejection? Courage isn't just for times when you're facing grievous danger. Any time you face difficult, unpredictable situations it takes courage to move forward. When you're tempted to turn away from your problems, let faith help you turn toward God. With Him you'll find the courage you need to do whatever needs to be done.

## DAY 35

# What's Your Motivation?

In preparing to play a role, an actress asks herself, "What's my character's motivation?" That's because what motivates us, moves us. If a character's desire is to be admired, rich, beautiful, or loved, that will influence her decisions and actions. As you allow God to work in and through you, your desires begin to fall in line with His own. There's no longer any need to act. You're free to be exactly who God created you to be.

### DAY 36
# Building Faith. . .Together

When women get together, there's usually a whole lot of talking going on. Conversing, counseling, giggling, and catching up on the latest news are all wonderful ways to build a friendship. But if you want to build your faith, take time to encourage one another. Tell your friends how you've seen God at work in their lives. Share what God's been teaching you. Ask questions. Pray. Praise. Your friendship will grow right along with your faith.

DAY 37

## Forget Not His Benefits

*Bless the LORD, O my soul: and all that is within me, bless his holy name. Bless the LORD, O my soul, and forget not all his benefits: who forgiveth all thine iniquities; who healeth all thy diseases; who redeemeth thy life from destruction; who crowneth thee with lovingkindness and tender mercies; who satisfieth thy mouth with good things; so that thy youth is renewed like the eagle's.*

PSALM 103:1–5 KJV

## DAY 38

### Expect the Unexpected

What can we expect from God? The unexpected. Many people who came to Jesus asked to be healed. But how Jesus healed them was never the same. He put mud on a blind man's eyes. A bleeding woman merely touched His robe. Sometimes, all Jesus did was speak—and healing happened. Coming to God in faith means you can expect that He will act. He promises He'll respond to your prayers. How? Anticipate the unexpected.

# DAY 39

## *Healing Faith*

*So Jesus and his followers stood up and went with the leader. Then a woman who had been bleeding for twelve years came behind Jesus and touched the edge of his coat. She was thinking, "If I can just touch his clothes, I will be healed." Jesus turned and saw the woman and said, "Be encouraged, dear woman. You are made well because you believed." And the woman was healed from that moment on.*

MATTHEW 9:19–22 NCV

## DAY 40
### Faith to Grow

God knows you inside and out. He knows how you feel, right here, right now. So why bother telling Him what's going on in your heart? Because that's how relationships grow. Sharing your personal struggles with a spouse or best friend is a sign of intimacy. It demonstrates your faith in that person's love for you. It also gives the other person an opportunity to offer comfort, help, and hope. God desires that same opportunity in your life.

## DAY 41

# Faith + Works

Works without faith are like a fish without water: It wants the element it should live in. A building without a basis cannot stand; faith is the foundation, and every good action is as a stone laid.

OWEN FELLTHAM

You do right when you offer faith to God; you do right when you offer works. But if you separate the two, then you do wrong. For faith without works is dead.

SAINT BERNARD OF CLAIRVAUX

DAY 42

## Pass It On

Has a faithful Bible teacher opened the Word to you? Maybe your church pastor or leader in a study group has touched your heart with the words of scripture, building your faith reserves or explaining a tricky passage that's never been clear before. Avoid leaving without appreciating the impact of that teaching on your thoughts and deeds. Support the person who brought you God's message—and somehow, pass it on to another who needs a blessing today.

DAY 43

# To God Be the Glory!

Want to fully experience God's perfect love? Then obey Him. When we walk the way Jesus did, we obey the Father. Instead of taking the glory for ourselves, we lift up the One who really deserves it, the One who reached down in love to save us when we were undeserving. God has been faithful through the generations and will continue to keep His promises through eternity. Let us be faithful to live our lives in honor of Him.

## DAY 44

### Just as God Says

"But now I urge you to keep up your courage, because not one of you will be lost; only the ship will be destroyed. Last night an angel of the God to whom I belong and whom I serve stood beside me and said, 'Do not be afraid, Paul. You must stand trial before Caesar; and God has graciously given you the lives of all who sail with you.' So keep up your courage, men, for I have faith in God that it will happen just as he told me."

ACTS 27:22–26 NIV

## DAY 45

### Lavish Love

God does not give His love in dribs and drabs. . . . God's love lets loose in our lives, filling them to the brim. Nothing is too good for His obedient children. He sacrificed His Son to make sons and daughters of sinners. Praise God that He loves you that much! Trust that His plans are for your good, that His will is always perfect. You can rest in the lavish love of your heavenly Father.

## DAY 46

# Generosity

In our culture it's considered admirable to pull yourself up by your own bootstraps—or kitten heel pumps, as the case may be. But God asks His children to walk together, leaning on one another for support. Being generous in sharing our time, our resources, and our experience helps God's family grow stronger as a whole. As we hold on loosely to what we've been given, our arms will be more able to hold on tightly to those around us.

## DAY 47

# All Grown Up

Teenage girls are known for being petty and cliquish. But you're all grown up now. You're not only a woman, you're a woman of faith. That means it's time to put away childish habits, especially those that keep you from loving others well. A true friend doesn't play games or hide behind masks. She's honest about who she is, open about her strengths, weaknesses, hopes, and fears. Her honesty invites others to be as authentic with her as she is with them.

## DAY 48

### Yield in Faith

*Father, this world can be a selfish place. It's easy to be drawn into a "me first" lifestyle—we spend so much time caring for ourselves while overlooking even those closest to us. Forgive me for getting so wrapped up in my desires that I fail to notice, let alone reach out to, those around me. May the deepest concern of my heart be that those whom I love will share heaven with Christ. Clarify Your Word, Father, that many may yield in faith. Amen.*

# Made to Order

When you're preparing a special meal, chances are you don't settle for "good enough." You rely on your favorite dishes, ones that look good, taste good, and are good for you. God feeds your soul similar spiritual fare. Like a good cook who consistently turns out good meals, our good God consistently bestows good gifts. Sometimes they're delectable delights. Other times they're much needed vegetables. You can trust in God's goodness to serve up exactly what you need.

# Surprised by Happiness

Faith is a journey. Like any journey, it's a mixed bag of experiences. You can celebrate grand vistas, then slog through bogs of mud—all in the same day. Though happiness is often dependent on circumstances, when your journey's guided by faith you can find yourself feeling happy at the most unexpected moments. Perhaps God brings a Bible verse to mind that encourages you. Maybe you see Him at work in a "coincidence." Where will God surprise you with happiness today?

## DAY 51

# For This Purpose

[Jesus said,] Rise, and stand upon thy feet: for I have appeared unto thee for this purpose, to make thee a minister and a witness both of these things which thou hast seen, and of those things in the which I will appear unto thee. . .unto whom now I send thee, to open their eyes, and to turn them from darkness to light, and from the power of Satan unto God, that they may receive forgiveness of sins, and inheritance among them which are sanctified by faith that is in me.

ACTS 26:16–18 KJV

## Faith for Real Life

Real life doesn't resemble what's seen on TV. Problems aren't resolved in an hour's time. There may be seasons where you need God's help just to make it through today. . .and tomorrow and the day after that. During times like these, God's presence can be a place of rest and refuge. Go for a walk. Draw a bubble bath. Find a quiet spot to just sit. Then invite God to join you. Allow Him to refresh you with His love.

# When No One's Watching

It's said that character is who you are in the dark. If integrity is part of that character, you'll do the right thing whether someone's watching or not. It takes faith to remain morally upright, honest, and true to your word in a culture where it's considered acceptable to do the exact opposite in the name of getting ahead. But God's way is ultimately the wisest, most beneficial way. Through your integrity, God may teach others lessons they'll never forget.

## DAY 54

*Take the Test*

*Examine yourselves to see whether you are in the faith; test yourselves. Do you not realize that Christ Jesus is in you—unless, of course, you fail the test? And I trust that you will discover that we have not failed the test. Now we pray to God that you will not do anything wrong—not so that people will see that we have stood the test but so that you will do what is right even though we may seem to have failed.*

2 Corinthians 13:5–7 niv

## DAY 55

# God's Kindness

A wise mother schools her children in the ways of kindness not only with her words but through her actions as well. God works the same way. Through the words of the Bible, God encourages His children to treat each other with respect, generosity, and consideration. But it's God's personal kindnesses to you that encourages your faith. Today, consider the many ways God has been kind to you just this week. What will your response be?

## DAY 56

# Hold Tight!

*My friends, watch out! Don't let evil thoughts
or doubts make any of you turn from the
living God. You must encourage one another
each day. And you must keep on while there
is still a time that can be called "today."
If you don't, then sin may fool some of you
and make you stubborn. We were sure about
Christ when we first became his people.
So let's hold tightly to our faith until the end.*

HEBREWS 3:12–14 CEV

DAY 57

*Never Alone*

Loneliness can make you feel like you're on a deserted island surrounded by a sea of people—yet no one notices you're there. But there is Someone who notices. Someone who'll never leave you. Someone who won't forget you or ignore you, no matter what you've done. You may be lonely, but you're never alone. Find a place of solace in the silence through prayer. Loneliness may be the perfect lifeline to draw you closer to God, the One whose love will never fail.

## Help along the Way

Carry each other's burdens, and in this way
you will fulfill the law of Christ.

GALATIANS 6:2 NIV

Father, in Your love and wisdom,
You've called us to support one another.
Throughout the ages You've placed faithful
people in Christians' lives who stand
beside them through life's triumphs and
tragedies. For King David this person
was Jonathan. Even Jesus had close
friends in Lazarus, Mary, and Martha.
Help me to be a faithful, loving,
and unforgettable friend. Amen.

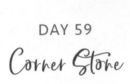

# DAY 59

## Corner Stone

*Wherefore also it is contained in the scripture, Behold, I lay in Sion a chief corner stone, elect, precious: and he that believeth on him shall not be confounded. Unto you therefore which believe he is precious: but unto them which be disobedient, the stone which the builders disallowed, the same is made the head of the corner, and a stone of stumbling, and a rock of offence, even to them which stumble at the word, being disobedient: whereunto also they were appointed.*

1 Peter 2:6–8 KJV

## DAY 60

### The Race of Faith

Faith is more like a marathon than a leisurely jog through the park. During some legs of the race you'll be feeling strong and confident. During others, you may find yourself stumbling over questions, losing sight of the right path, or wanting to sit on the sidelines. To keep moving forward, run the race of faith one step at a time. Consider each day a fresh starting line. Moment by moment, with God's help, you will persevere.

# DAY 61

## Keep in Line

Faith keeps our prayers in line with the truth behind what we say we believe. If we believe God loves us, believe Jesus is who He said He was, believe God has a plan for our lives, believe He's good, wise, and just—our prayers will reflect these beliefs. They'll be in line with God's will—with what God desires for our lives. These are the kind of prayers God assures us He'll answer, in His time and His way.

## DAY 62

# A Singular Purpose

"Did you do that on purpose?" Any mom who asks a child this question should be ready to carefully weigh the answer. But how about you? Consider what you've done this week. How much of it was truly "on purpose"? Faith provides a singular purpose for living: to love God and others. Fulfilling this purpose requires living prayerfully and with intention. Today, ask God to help slow you down. Consider your true purpose as you make your plans.

## DAY 63

# Faithfully Obey

It is a land the LORD your God cares for;
the eyes of the LORD your God are continually
on it from the beginning of the year to its
end. So if you faithfully obey the commands
I am giving you today—to love the LORD your
God and to serve him with all your heart
and with all your soul—then I will send rain
on your land in its season, both autumn
and spring rains, so that you may gather
in your grain, new wine and olive oil.

DEUTERONOMY 11:12–14 NIV

# DAY 64

## A Time to Rest

For three years, Jesus devoted his life to spreading the Good News about God's love. This was an incredibly important job, one with eternal consequences. But even Jesus took time to rest. Although He dined with friends, taught, preached, and performed miracles, many times he left spiritually hungry crowds behind to spend time alone with His heavenly Father. You have many important roles to fill in this life. Rest is one of God's gifts that can empower you to accomplish what He's given you to do.

## DAY 65

# Something Good

It's easy to focus solely on the glorious benefits of believing in God. Gifts like forgiveness, eternal life, a fresh start, and unconditional love are certainly worth celebrating. But each of these gifts comes at a very high cost. Jesus paid for them with His life. Jesus' sacrifice involved physical suffering, humiliation, betrayal, and separation from His Father. Choosing to follow Jesus in a life of faith will involve sacrifice on your part. Allow Him to show you how sacrifice can lead to something good.

# DAY 66
## The Light

Jesus said, "For a brief time still, the light is among you. Walk by the light you have so darkness doesn't destroy you. If you walk in darkness, you don't know where you're going. As you have the light, believe in the light. Then the light will be within you, and shining through your lives. You'll be children of light." . . . All these God-signs he had given them and they still didn't get it, still wouldn't trust him.

JOHN 12:35–37 MSG

## The Big Picture

Abraham wholeheartedly believed in God's power and love. So, when God told Abraham to sacrifice his long-awaited son, Abraham prepared to do exactly what God asked. Surely Abraham had questions. He didn't know how everything would turn out. In the end, God saved Isaac and commended Abraham's faith. Serving God isn't always an easy path. You may not see the big picture behind what you're asked to do. But you can trust God's plan for you is good.

## DAY 68

## Healthy Eyes

*No man, when he hath lighted a candle, putteth it in a secret place, neither under a bushel, but on a candlestick, that they which come in may see the light. The light of the body is the eye: therefore when thine eye is single, thy whole body also is full of light; but when thine eye is evil, thy body also is full of darkness. Take heed therefore that the light which is in thee be not darkness.*

LUKE 11:33–35 KJV

DAY 69

## Always Awake

For small children, bedtime can be a scary time. They may be afraid of the dark, of monsters lurking under their bed, or of bad dreams disturbing their slumber. Bedtime prayers can help calm their fears. They can calm yours as well. Knowing God never sleeps can help you sleep more soundly. If you're in the dark about a certain situation, if "monsters" are threatening your peace, take your concerns to God. It's never too late to call out to Him.

## When Darkness Comes

It is blessed when we can praise God when the sun has gone down, when darkness lowers and trials multiply. Faith does not struggle; faith lets God do it all.

CORRIE TEN BOOM

When you come to the edge of all the light you know and are about ready to step off into the darkness of the unknown, faith is knowing one of two things will happen: there will be something solid to stand on, or you will be taught how to fly.

BARBARA J. WINTER

# DAY 71

## Upheld

*What incredible faith Job displayed, Lord!
His life was filled with blessings—sons
and daughters, many servants, and much
livestock. This of course was life as Job used
to know it, before his character was tested.
His life became an unwelcome ride on a
trolley called tragedy. And through all of this
Job refused to blame You or to sin. I wonder
if my faith would remain as strong if tested
as sharply as Job's. But one thing is certain,
Lord. You will remain steadfast. . .and
You will uphold my faith. Amen.*

## DAY 72

### Step by Step

Picture yourself in a race, struggling to reach the finish line. You're exhausted, discouraged, perhaps even injured. You're tempted to give up. Then a friend runs onto the course from the sidelines. She places her arm around your waist, inviting you to lean on her for strength and support. Together, step by step, you see the race to completion. God is that kind of friend. Whether the strength you need today is physical, emotional, or spiritual, God is there. Lean on Him.

# Number the Stars

And, behold, the word of the LORD came
unto him, saying, This shall not be thine heir;
but he that shall come forth out of thine own
bowels shall be thine heir. And he brought
him forth abroad, and said, Look now toward
heaven, and tell the stars, if thou be able to
number them: and he said unto him, So shall
thy seed be. And he believed in the LORD;
and he counted it to him for righteousness.

GENESIS 15:4–6 KJV

## Flip the Switch

Some trains of thought need to be derailed. That's because they don't lead you closer to God and grow your faith. But like a switch operator who changes the track a train is on to save it from disaster, you can change the direction of your thoughts. If others could read your mind, and you'd be embarrassed by what they read, flip the switch. Choose to focus on something worthy of your time and God's praise.

## DAY 75

# Wholly True

The truth can't be twisted or stretched. It can't masquerade as a "half" truth or a "little white lie." If what you say isn't wholly true, it isn't the truth. Period. Speaking the truth doesn't mean saying aloud every thought that enters your head. It means living your faith out through your words. It means passing out words like gifts. Choose each one carefully. Then wrap them in love and respect. Be as honest and truthful with others as God has been with you.

## Faithful Work

Your faith should affect your work—in wonderfully positive ways. Whether you work outside the home or not, whether you love your job or are doing it simply to pay the bills, tackle every job as if you were doing it for God Himself. Be honest, diligent, and gracious. Give yourself wholeheartedly to the task at hand, no matter how small. Give God your best by doing your best. He gave His best for you.

# DAY 77

## The Great Commission

*Afterward he appeared unto the eleven
as they sat at meat, and upbraided them
with their unbelief and hardness of heart,
because they believed not them which
had seen him after he was risen. And he
said unto them, Go ye into all the world,
and preach the gospel to every creature.
He that believeth and is baptized shall
be saved; but he that believeth not
shall be damned. And these signs
shall follow them that believe.*

MARK 16:14–17 KJV

## Family Time

Moms wear many hats. They're called to be chefs, teachers, maids, nurses, mediators, and activity directors—sometimes all in the same 24-hour period. But God has entrusted you with an even more important role in your family. You're a spiritual leader. As you live out your faith, share the "whys" behind what you do. Point your children in directions that will lead them closer to God. If you aren't a mom, seek out ways to mentor the younger generation in your church family. Your strong faith helps build a stronger family.

## A Parting Gift

When attending a going away party, it's customary to give a gift to the one who's going away. Jesus turned this concept on its head, as He so often did with the status quo. At the Last Supper, the day before He died, Jesus gave all of His followers a gift—peace. When you choose to follow Jesus in a life of faith, you receive this gift. You'll find it fits your life perfectly, complementing any and every circumstance.

## More Dependable

The test of our faith in the promises of God is never found in the easygoing, comfortable ways of life, but in the great emergencies, the times of storm and of stress, the days of adversity, when all human aid fails.

ETHEL BELL

Never, never pin your whole faith on any human being: not if he is the best and wisest in the whole world. There are lots of nice things you can do with sand; but do not try building a house on it.

C. S. LEWIS

DAY 81

*Partner in Life*

You've probably heard the expression "carry the weight of the world on your shoulders." Does this ring true in your life? Take heart! What God has called you to accomplish in your life, He has not called you to accomplish alone. He is always there, providing you with the resources you need to get the job done. . . . Whether you need wisdom, inspiration, confidence, strength, or just plain tenacity, you will find your answer in Him.

# DAY 82

## Grafted In

*Thou, being a wild olive tree, wert grafted in among them, and with them partakest of the root and fatness of the olive tree; boast not against the branches. But if thou boast, thou bearest not the root, but the root thee. Thou wilt say then, The branches were broken off, that I might be grafted in. Well; because of unbelief they were broken off, and thou standest by faith. Be not highminded, but fear: for if God spared not the natural branches, take heed lest he also spare not thee.*

ROMANS 11:17–21 KJV

## DAY 83

# Cries for Help

There's probably no more common prayer than the word "help." Even those who aren't aware they're calling out to the living God, cry out for help in times of despair, fear, or pain. But you know God is near. You know He hears. In faith, you believe He will help. Regardless of your circumstance—big or small—don't wait until you come to the end of your rope to pray. Call out to Him anytime, anywhere.

## DAY 84
### Hope of Heaven

The Bible says we will encounter trials in this life. After all, this world is not our home; it's just a temporary residence. Though you're not home in heaven yet, that doesn't mean its existence isn't relevant to you right now. Holding on to your hope of heaven gives you an eternal perspective. It frees you from the fear of death, inspires you to tell others about God's everlasting love, and reminds you that no matter what you face in this life, you're guaranteed a happy ending.

DAY 85

*First in the Future*

Jesus said, "I tell you the truth, all those who have left houses, brothers, sisters, mother, father, children, or farms for me and for the Good News will get more than they left. Here in this world they will have a hundred times more homes, brothers, sisters, mothers, children, and fields. And with those things, they will also suffer for their belief. But in this age they will have life forever. Many who are first now will be last in the future. And many who are last now will be first in the future."

MARK 10:29–31 NCV

DAY 86

## Testing, 1, 2, 3. . .

As a kid, you took plenty of tests. Your GPA was determined by how your efforts measured up to a set standard. As Christians, we're told to take another test: "Test yourselves and find out if you really are true to your faith" (2 Corinthians 13:5 CEV). Measure your character against the person God desires you to become. This isn't a test God grades. It's simply a tool to help you know where your faith needs to grow. Best of all, this is a group project. Jesus is working both in you and through you.

## DAY 87

# In Christ Alone

Savings accounts, insurance, family. . .where does your faith rest when times are tough? Who will be your salvation when all else fails? If our faith is in Christ, we are established upon firm ground. We are braced against any storm, upheld by our loving and infallible God. But if our faith is in systems, people, or even religion, it's doomed to fail. Take stock of your faith today. Are you relying on worldly power, or are you placing your trust in Christ alone?

## Sown Seed

*Now the parable is this: The seed is the word of God. . . . And that which fell among thorns are they, which, when they have heard, go forth, and are choked with cares and riches and pleasures of this life, and bring no fruit to perfection. But that on the good ground are they, which in an honest and good heart, having heard the word, keep it, and bring forth fruit with patience.*

LUKE 8:11, 14–15 KJV

## DAY 89
### Let Love Shine

What mountain are you facing today? Perhaps it's the reconciliation of a relationship. Or maybe it's just that pile of laundry you've neglected. Whatever it is, it would be nice to simply "pray it away." But faith isn't a gift God gives to make life easier. Faith is God's classroom in which we learn how to become more loving—more like God Himself. Ask God to let love shine through in everything you do. Even sorting socks.

# Whale, That'll Get My Attention!

Lord, You solicited Jonah's help in bringing a message to Ninevah. But Jonah's fear of the Ninevites loomed far greater than his fear of You. He finally responded in faith— after an incredible display of Your power. Even though I shake my head at Jonah's stubborness, I know I reflect his attitude in my own life at times. Please help me yield in the areas You're ready to work on in my life—before it takes a whale to bend my knees to Your will! Amen.

# Forgiveness

When you put your faith in God, the very first thing He does is forgive you. He doesn't overlook what you've done. He forgives it. Immediately. Completely. Eternally. Choosing to follow His example isn't always easy. But it's always right. When others offend you, don't let your forgiveness hinge on their apology or repentance. You can wisely set boundaries and still offer forgiveness. Ask God to help you forgive before another's fault can fester into a painful, distracting grudge.

## DAY 92

## Faithful Reward

God knows your heart. Even when you feel invisible to the world and that your faith is for naught, don't lose heart. The One who holds the future in His hands sees your faithfulness. He has entrusted you with much responsibility because He knows He can count on you. He will reward you and will bring you into a place of blessing. Expect it and believe He'll do it. God applauds your faith in Him!

DAY 93

## Refreshed

Busy schedules, challenging tasks, endless responsibilities. . .it's easy to feel worn down, especially when our faith takes a back seat to life's demands. God has promised you strength for your days—even the toughest ones. He is the source you can draw on when you feel your supply is running low. Reach out to Him in faith—He is faithful to keep His promises. You don't have to go at life alone. When you reach for Him, He's always there, ready to refresh you.

## DAY 94

# Woman, Believe!

*Jesus saith unto her, Woman, believe me. . . the hour cometh, and now is, when the true worshippers shall worship the Father in spirit and in truth: for the Father seeketh such to worship him. God is a Spirit: and they that worship him must worship him in spirit and in truth. . . . The woman then left her waterpot, and went her way into the city, and saith to the men, Come, see a man, which told me all things that ever I did: is not this the Christ?*

JOHN 4:21, 23–24, 28–29 KJV

## Above and Beyond

In Jesus' day, the people of Israel were looking for the Messiah promised in scripture. They believed this Savior would restore Israel to its former power and prosperity. Jesus didn't meet their expectations. He exceeded them. Jesus offered them an abundance of riches that couldn't be stolen or lose value: true treasures like joy, peace, forgiveness, and eternal life. Jesus offers these same treasures to you. All you need to do is place your faith in Him.

# A Shield of Faith

Some women keep their faith tucked away like a family heirloom, displaying it only on holidays like Easter and Christmas. But if you truly believe what God says is true, faith will be part of your everyday life. Faith is more than words of comfort. It's a shield that can protect you from an assault of doubt or the temptation to do something you know goes against what God's planned for you. Take faith with you wherever you go.

## DAY 97

# Spirit of Faith

For we which live are always delivered unto death for Jesus' sake, that the life also of Jesus might be made manifest in our mortal flesh. So then death worketh in us, but life in you. We having the same spirit of faith, according as it is written, I believed, and therefore have I spoken; we also believe, and therefore speak; knowing that he which raised up the Lord Jesus shall raise up us also by Jesus, and shall present us with you.

2 Corinthians 4:11–14 kjv

## Guiding Light

Lord, teach me the wisdom of faith. Faith is the radar that sees through the fog the reality of things at a distance that the human eye cannot see.

CORRIE TEN BOOM

Faith looks up and sails on. . .not seeing one shoreline or earthly lighthouse. . . . Often our way seems to lead into utter uncertainty or even darkness and disaster. But He opens the way, making our midnight hours the very gates of day.

A. B. SIMPSON

## DAY 99

### *Life Letter*

The Bible is like a letter from your best friend. In it, God shares how much He loves you, what He's been up to since the creation of the world, and His plans for the future. You're an important part of those plans. The life you live through faith is the letter you write in return. But others will also sneak a peek at your "life letter." The life you live may be the only Bible some people ever read.

## Ultimate Makeover

You're no longer the woman you once were. When you put your faith in God, you experience the ultimate makeover. You're totally forgiven. You're empowered to be able to do whatever God asks. Your old habits lose their grip over you. But continued growth and change is a joint effort between you and God. If there's any area in your life that seems resistant to change, talk to God about it right now—and every morning until change takes place.

# DAY 101

## Please God

This is what the Scriptures mean by saying, "Abraham had faith in God, and God was pleased with him." That's how Abraham became God's friend. You can now see that we please God by what we do and not only by what we believe. For example, Rahab had been a prostitute. But she pleased God when she welcomed the spies and sent them home by another way. Anyone who doesn't breathe is dead, and faith that doesn't do anything is just as dead!

JAMES 2:23–26 CEV

# Gardener of Souls

Some women have a bona fide green thumb. They take a seemingly dead stick and nurture it into a verdant piece of paradise. Consider how ridiculous it would be for that once sickly stick to brag to his foliage friends about the great turnaround he'd accomplished in his own life. Obviously, all credit goes to the gardener. God is the ultimate gardener. His focus is tending His children. Humbly allow Him to have His way in helping your faith grow.

## DAY 103

# Faith Is the Key

Death is a part of life, at least on this earth. But because of Jesus, death is not something to be feared. It's a door leading from this life into the next. Faith is the key that opens that door. Whenever this life leaves you questioning, hurting, or longing for heaven, picture yourself fingering that key. The more tightly you hold on to your faith, the more peace, hope, and joy you'll experience on this side of that door.

DAY 104

## Because of You

The thought of God praising you may be a new one. But when Jesus returns, what you've done and overcome because of your faith will be visible to all. But it's not the accolades of others that make this worth anticipating. It's the chance to see God smile—and know it's because of you. In this life, you may feel your efforts go unnoticed. Rejoice in knowing God sees, and praises, everything you do because of your faith in Him.

## Resurrection and Life

Martha saith unto him, I know that he shall
rise again in the resurrection at the last day.
Jesus said unto her, I am the resurrection,
and the life: he that believeth in me,
though he were dead, yet shall he live:
and whosoever liveth and believeth in
me shall never die. Believest thou this?
She saith unto him, Yea, Lord: I believe
that thou art the Christ, the Son of God,
which should come into the world.

JOHN 11:24–27 KJV

## DAY 106
## *Rock of Faith*

*The L<small>ORD</small> is my rock, and my fortress, and
my deliverer; the God of my rock; in him will
I trust: he is my shield, and the horn of my
salvation, my high tower, and my refuge,
my saviour; thou savest me from violence.*

2 S<small>AMUEL</small> 22:2–3 KJV

*What faithful words of David, Lord! How
they paint a picture of the peace, comfort,
and security we seek for our lives. I praise
You only, Jesus, my Rock of faith
and redeemer. Amen.*

## Beyond Basics

*Need* is an easy word to use—and abuse. "I need new shoes to go with this outfit." "I need chocolate, right here, right now!" "I need some respect!" When God says He'll provide what we need, it's always on His terms, not ours. He provides everything we need to do everything He's asked us to do. Yet our loving God goes far beyond supplying the basics. He surprises us by filling to overflowing needs we never even knew we had.

DAY 108

*Gold Crowns*

Exactly how God rewards His children is a bit of a mystery. The Bible tells us we'll receive gold crowns in heaven, which we'll promptly cast at Jesus' feet to honor Him. But the Bible also talks about rewards in this life. Our rewards may be delivered in tangible ways, such as through success or financial gain. But our reward may also be a more intangible treasure, such as contentment and joy. Treasures like these will never tarnish or grow old.

## Through Rivers

Tried faith brings experience. You could not have believed your own weakness had you not been compelled to pass through the rivers; and you would never have known God's strength had you not been supported amid the water-floods. Faith expects from God what is beyond all expectation.

ANDREW MURRAY

All providences are doors to trial. Men have drowned in seas of prosperity as well as in rivers of affliction. Real, true faith is man's weakness leaning on God's strength.

D. L. MOODY

## DAY 110

### Fear God

Fear sounds like a rather dubious route to take to find security. After all, you wouldn't hire a personal bodyguard you feared would harm you. But fearing God isn't the same as being afraid of Him. Fearing God means standing in awe of Him. After all, He's the almighty Creator, our sovereign Master, the righteous Judge of all. But this all-powerful God is *for* you. He's on your side, fighting on your behalf. Talk about the ultimate bodyguard!

## DAY 111

### Believe Boldly

*After a few days, Jesus returned to
Capernaum, and word got around that he
was back home. A crowd gathered, jamming
the entrance so no one could get in or out.
He was teaching the Word. They brought
a paraplegic to him, carried by four men.
When they weren't able to get in because
of the crowd, they removed part of the roof
and lowered the paraplegic on his stretcher.
Impressed by their bold belief, Jesus said to
the paraplegic, "Son, I forgive your sins."*

MARK 2:1–5 MSG

## DAY 112

### A Story to Tell

For some people, faith is a very private part of their lives. But you have a story to tell that others need to hear. Sharing how God is at work in your life gives others permission to ask spiritual questions. Don't worry about not having all the answers. You can't. An infinite God will always be bigger than our finite minds can comprehend. But saying aloud what you believe is part of living, and growing, in your faith.

DAY 113

## It Takes Effort

Some people confuse luck with success. They want the reward of a successful life without having to put in the work. But success is something that's achieved over time. Whether it's in the workplace, parenting your children, or growing in your faith, success is the result of consistent effort toward reaching a goal. A successful life is made up of successful days—and a truly successful day is one that draws you closer to God and His plans for you.

## DAY 114

# Consider What He's Done

*[Samuel said,] For the LORD will not forsake his people for his great name's sake: because it hath pleased the LORD to make you his people. . . . I will teach you the good and the right way: only fear the LORD, and serve him in truth with all your heart: for consider how great things he hath done for you. But if ye shall still do wickedly, ye shall be consumed.*

1 SAMUEL 12:22–25 KJV

## Jesus Is the Way

Believing all good people go to heaven sounds nice. But it doesn't make sense when you consider it. How do you measure goodness? Where's the cutoff between being "in" and being "out"? Spiritual truth cannot be relative or change according to how we feel. It must be timeless, steadfast—like Jesus. Jesus said that putting our faith in Him is the only way we can be reconciled with God and receive eternal life. Trust the truth. Trust Jesus.

## DAY 116

# Incomparably Wise

Only God sees the big picture of your life in the context of the past, the present, and the future. He not only sees this picture, He has the power to transform it. In addition, God is incomparably wise, so He knows the best way this transformation can be accomplished. Trusting God with your life shows wisdom on your part. The more closely you follow where He leads, the more your own wisdom will grow.

## Strengthened

Lord God, I love reading the apostle Paul's
letters to Timothy. They are filled with advice
and overflow with Paul's concern for his
"son in the faith." Paul had to make sure
that Timothy remained strong in the faith.
For Timothy would now "carry the torch
of faith" and continue bringing the Gospel
to all who would listen. Like Timothy,
use me, Lord, to do Your will. May I find
strength in Your Word as Timothy no
doubt found strength. Amen.

## DAY 118

# Run the Race

*Wherefore seeing we also are compassed about with so great a cloud of witnesses, let us lay aside every weight, and the sin which doth so easily beset us, and let us run with patience the race that is set before us, looking unto Jesus the author and finisher of our faith; who for the joy that was set before him endured the cross, despising the shame, and is set down at the right hand of the throne of God.*

HEBREWS 12:1–2 KJV

# Drink Deep

Kindness is the quiet compassion that flows from a loving heart. It doesn't announce its actions with shouts of "Look at me! Look what I did!" It whispers ever so gently, "Look at you. You're so worthy of love. Caring for you is my pleasure, my delight." Being the focus of an almighty King's kindness can be incredibly humbling, as well as encouraging. Let both humility and joy foster gratitude—and growth—in you. "Drink deep of God's pure kindness" as your faith matures (1 Peter 2:2–3 MSG).

## DAY 120

*Walk with Him*

Being single by choice feels different than being single by circumstance. If you deeply desire to be married, or if your spouse has passed away, you may struggle with feelings of loneliness, discontent, and even resentment toward God. If these feelings arise, don't bury yourself in them. Take them straight to God. Honestly tell Him how you feel. God loves you like a Father, Friend, Lover, Husband, and Deliverer. Walk with Him. He'll lead you toward healing and wholeness. Have faith in His perfect plan for your life.

## DAY 121

# Faithfully Wait

Yet this I call to mind and therefore I have hope: Because of the LORD's great love we are not consumed, for his compassions never fail. They are new every morning; great is your faithfulness. I say to myself, "The LORD is my portion; therefore I will wait for him." The LORD is good to those whose hope is in him, to the one who seeks him; it is good to wait quietly for the salvation of the LORD.

LAMENTATIONS 3:21–26 NIV

## DAY 122

# Reaching Out in Care

From celebrities to nobodies, atheists to those martyred for their faith, all people matter to God. It's easy to only invest yourself in relationships that feel comfortable and personally beneficial. But faith sees beyond social circles and stereotypes. Ask God to help you reach beyond your relational comfort zone. Reaching out tells someone you care. It means that person matters. Know that God's help in your life means the very same thing. He cares for you because He cares *about* you. Let that fact encourage you in your faith today.

## DAY 123

# *Fresh Start*

We all blow it. We let anger turn our words into weapons. We fall back into patterns we vowed we'd never repeat. But this is another minute, another morning, another chance to begin anew. Remember, "The LORD's love never ends; his mercies never stop. They are new every morning" (Lamentations 3:22–23 NCV). Faith can break a cycle of regrettable yesterdays—if we let it. God offers forgiveness and a fresh start to all who ask. He never tires of us bringing our brokenness to Him.

## DAY 124

*Add to This*

Whereby are given unto us exceeding great and precious promises: that by these ye might be partakers of the divine nature. . . . And beside this, giving all diligence, add to your faith virtue; and to virtue knowledge; and to knowledge temperance; and to temperance patience; and to patience godliness; and to godliness brotherly kindness; and to brotherly kindness charity. For if these things be in you, and abound, they make you that ye shall neither be barren nor unfruitful in the knowledge of our Lord Jesus Christ.

2 PETER 1:4–8 KJV

DAY 125

## God First

"Seek ye first the kingdom of God, and his righteousness." (Matthew 6:33 KJV). Putting God first sounds like the right thing to do. But what does that look like in real life? Does it mean spending every moment reading the Bible or praying over questions like, "Paper or plastic?" Holding God's kingdom as your top priority simply means that God's way becomes your way. Each day, ask God to help you live, and love, in a way that makes Him proud.

# Who Is He?

"Who do you say I am?" (Matthew 16:15 NIV). Jesus repeatedly asked this question to those who followed after Him. He knew that in a short while He would be gone, and all these fledgling Christians would have to bolster their faith with His words and actions. Jesus wanted to be sure they would not allow the world's viewpoint to diminish who He was. Jesus' question is no less important for us today. How we view God is *vitally* important. So, who do you say He is?

## Special Access

God's best gifts, like valuable jewels, are kept under lock and key, and those who want them must, with fervent faith, importunately ask for them; for God is a rewarder of them that diligently seek Him.

D. L. MOODY

Christian faith is a grand cathedral, with divinely pictured windows. Standing without, you see no glory, nor can imagine any. But standing within, every ray of light reveals a harmony of unspeakable splendors.

NATHANIEL HAWTHORNE

# The Best Plan

When people mention "the best laid plans," they're usually bemoaning how the unexpected derailed what once seemed like a sure thing. God's the master of the unexpected. That doesn't mean planning is a bad thing. It helps us use time, money, and resources in a more efficient way. But the only plans that are set in stone are God's own. Make sure your plans are in line with God's purposes. Then have faith that His will is always best.

DAY 129

*Warming Hearts*

*God's glory is on tour in the skies, God-craft on exhibit across the horizon. . . . God makes a huge dome for the sun—a superdome! The morning sun's a new husband leaping from his honeymoon bed, the daybreaking sun an athlete racing to the tape. That's how God's Word vaults across the skies from sunrise to sunset, melting ice, scorching deserts, warming hearts to faith.*

PSALM 19:1, 4–6 MSG

## Say Yes

Faith gives you the desire—and power—to do things you may have never even dreamed of attempting before. Serving meals to the homeless. Leading a Bible study. Praying for an ailing coworker. Sharing your personal story aloud in church. Forgiving someone who's betrayed you. The more you grow in your faith, the more God will stretch your idea of who you are—and what you can do. Through God's power, you can confidently say, "Yes!" to doing anything He asks.

## DAY 131

# Deep Satisfaction

You know the feeling. You've worked long and hard to finish a project, and you've finally reached the end. You've done well; you're satisfied. Satisfaction is the result of a job well done. Sometimes your expectation for the blessings of God requires you to press a little harder and stretch your faith a little farther to see the results you've asked God for. You can be sure all your effort will be rewarded. God promises to satisfy your soul—a deep satisfaction only He can provide.

# DAY 132
## Waiting and Watching

"Everything you ask for in prayer will be yours, if you only have faith" (Mark 11:24 CEV). How exciting to know that what you've asked God for is on its way. As God works behind the scenes to bring about everything you're waiting for, your faith is at work preparing for the arrival of His blessing. Just remember, His timing is perfect, and His will best. Keep strong in your faith; God will not disappoint those whose hearts are His.

# DAY 133

## Rooted and Built Up

For though I be absent in the flesh, yet am I with you in the spirit, joying and beholding your order, and the stedfastness of your faith in Christ. As ye have therefore received Christ Jesus the Lord, so walk ye in him: rooted and built up in him, and stablished in the faith, as ye have been taught, abounding therein with thanksgiving. Beware lest any man spoil you through philosophy and vain deceit, after the tradition of men, after the rudiments of the world, and not after Christ.

Colossians 2:5–8 KJV

## Just as You Are

God accepts you completely. You don't need to clean up your language, change your lifestyle, or step inside of a church. Once you put your faith in Jesus, things between you and God are made right. Period. But acceptance is only the first step in this relationship. As God's Spirit continues working in your heart, He gives you the desire and strength you need to mature into who you were created to be—an amazing child of God whose character reflects the Father.

# Spiritual Armor

A woman donning armor brings to mind images of Xena the Warrior Princess or Joan of Arc. But the armor God offers is neither fantasy nor outdated. It's a spiritual arsenal of offensive and defensive gear. It's comprised of weapons such as truth, righteousness, peace, and faith. There's a battle going on every day for your mind and heart. But there's no reason to be afraid. Through faith, God's given you everything you need to be victorious.

## DAY 136

# Faithful Abraham

*This only would I learn of you, Received
ye the Spirit by the works of the law, or by
the hearing of faith? . . . Even as Abraham
believed God, and it was accounted to him
for righteousness. Know ye therefore that
they which are of faith, the same are the
children of Abraham. And the scripture,
foreseeing that God would justify the
heathen through faith, preached before
the gospel unto Abraham, saying, In thee
shall all nations be blessed. So then
they which be of faith are blessed
with faithful Abraham.*

GALATIANS 3:2, 6–9 KJV

# Faithful to Change

What you believe will influence the choices you make. If you believe in gravity, you won't jump from a seventh story balcony to save time in getting to your hair appointment. If you believe what Jesus says, you'll change the way you live. Jesus often talks about the importance of traits such as honesty, purity, and generosity. Though God's Spirit helps change your heart, it's the daily choices you make that help bring traits like these to maturity.

## DAY 138

# Worry Reliever

Sometimes it feels like it's a woman's job to worry. If you can't be assured that all of your loved ones' physical and emotional needs are being met, fretting about them makes you feel involved—like you're loving them, even if you're powerless to help. But you know Someone who does have the power to help. Anytime you feel the weight of worry, whether it's over someone else's problems or your own, let faith relieve you of the burden. Turn your worries into prayers.

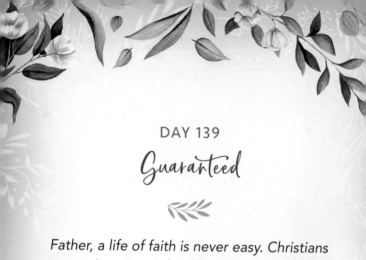

## DAY 139

*Guaranteed*

Father, a life of faith is never easy. Christians are not immune to hardship; in fact, trouble is guaranteed! To nonbelievers, faith may even seem foolish. They cannot see Your beauty or comprehend the blessings that flow from being faithful to You. But I see Your wonders each day. I remember the times You've reached out in Your glory to strengthen me. Fill me with Your splendor anew that I may never become blind to the richness of my faith. Amen.

## DAY 140

# Family Resemblance

Moms pass on lots of things to their children, like the shape of their nose or color of their eyes. They can also pass on things like speech patterns or lifestyle preferences. That's because when you spend time together, you pick up the habits of those you're with. In the same way, the more time you spend with God meditating on His Word and praying, the more your character begins to resemble His. That's a family resemblance worth celebrating.

# DAY 141

## The Science of Faith

Science has sometimes been said to be opposed to faith, and inconsistent with it. But all science, in fact, rests on a basis of faith, for it assumes the permanence and uniformity of natural laws—a thing which can never be demonstrated.

TRYON EDWARDS

He goes not amiss who goes in the company of God. Every man lives by faith, the nonbeliever as well as the saint; the one by faith in natural laws and the other by faith in God.

A. W. TOZER

DAY 142

*In Style*

Before you leave the house, chances are you make sure you're appropriately dressed. You don't go to a business meeting in your pj's, to the grocery store in your swimsuit, or off for a jog in heels. Faith offers you a different kind of wardrobe, one that's appropriate for every occasion. By clothing yourself in compassion, you reflect God's very own style—a style that always looks good on you and compliments everyone you meet.

## DAY 143

# Faith to Be Content

Being content with what you have is one thing. Being content with who you are is quite another. This kind of contentment isn't complacency. It doesn't negate the importance of striving for excellence or encouraging growth and change. It means being at peace with the way God designed you and the life He's given you. This kind of contentment is only available in daily doses. Through faith, seek God and His path to contentment each and every morning.

## DAY 144
# For Philemon

*Philemon, each time I mention you in my prayers, I thank God. I hear about your faith in our Lord Jesus and about your love for all of God's people. As you share your faith with others, I pray that they may come to know all the blessings Christ has given us. My friend, your love has made me happy and has greatly encouraged me. It has also cheered the hearts of God's people.*

PHILEMON 1:4–7 CEV

## DAY 145

### Moving Faith

The time we set aside to read the Bible and pray each day is often called "daily devotions." Have you ever considered why? Think about what it means to be devoted. Devotion is the commitment of yourself to something or someone you love. The same is true with spiritual devotion. Your spiritual faith is a commitment to love God. And since the word *love* is a verb, an action word, your devotion to God is faith on the move. Where will faith move you today?

## No Stopping You Now!

Eternal life doesn't begin after you die. It begins the day you put your faith in Jesus' love. Right now, you're in the childhood of eternity. You're learning and growing. Like a toddler trying to master the art of walking, you may wobble a bit at times. But if you fall, God helps get you back on your feet again. Once your faith sets you on the path toward heaven, nothing—absolutely nothing—can prevent you from reaching your destination.

DAY 147

## More Precious Than Gold

*These troubles come to prove that your faith is pure. This purity of faith is worth more than gold, which can be proved to be pure by fire but will ruin. But the purity of your faith will bring you praise and glory and honor when Jesus Christ is shown to you. You have not seen Christ, but still you love him. You cannot see him now, but you believe in him. So you are filled with a joy that cannot be explained, a joy full of glory.*

1 Peter 1:7–8 NCV

## DAY 148

### Faithful Companion

Dogs are known as "man's best friend." That's because dogs are faithful. They don't hold a grudge or get so preoccupied with their own lives that they forget to greet you at the door. That kind of loyalty comes easy to a dog. But for complex human beings it takes an act of will— and heart. With God's help, you can become someone that others can depend on. Including God. Live out your faith by becoming more faithful.

## DAY 149

## East to West

Lord, sometimes the hardest thing to grasp in my faith walk is forgiveness. How a holy God would sacrifice so much for sinners, so that we might have forgiveness of those sins. You promise to remove my sin "as far as the east is from the west" (Psalm 103:12 KJV). Lord, forgive me, no matter what my sin, that I might turn from it and faithfully serve You. Help me declare Your great forgiveness to others. Amen.

# DAY 150

## *Not Seen*

*Now faith is confidence in what we hope
for and assurance about what we do not see.
This is what the ancients were commended
for. By faith we understand that the universe
was formed at God's command, so that what
is seen was not made out of what was visible.
By faith Abel brought God a better offering
than Cain did. By faith he was commended
as righteous, when God spoke well of his
offerings. And by faith Abel still speaks,
even though he is dead.*

HEBREWS 11:1–4 NIV

# DAY 151

## Through Faith

But God has a way to make people right
with him without the law, and he has now
shown us that way which the law and the
prophets told us about. God makes people
right with himself through their faith in
Jesus Christ. This is true for all who believe
in Christ, because all people are the same:
Everyone has sinned and fallen short of
God's glorious standard, and all need to
be made right with God by his
grace, which is a free gift.

ROMANS 3:21–24 NCV

## DAY 152

## Tend the Fruit

A Christian who doesn't spend much time with the Savior bears little fruit. Faith shrivels under the heat of life's sun and lack of spiritual water. But a believer who taps into Him every day, spending time talking and listening to Him, through prayer and the Word, begins to burgeon with it. Faith blossoms; roots run deep into firm ground. Opportunities to reach out will come, and the fruit will become heavier all the time.

DAY 153

## Rain or Shine

The weather is not ours to control, but God's. We need to give thanks for the daily blessings God offers us—rain that keeps wells and reservoirs filled or sunshine for a special outing. When the weather doesn't go "our way," we can still thank God that He's in control. The same is true in our lives. Through ups and downs, God is in control. Through thick and thin, God is in control. Thank Him for His faithfulness today.

## DAY 154

# Pray in Faith

Faith is to the soul what life is to the body. Prayer is to faith what breath is to the body. How a person can live and not breathe is past my comprehension, and how a person can believe and not pray is past my comprehension too.

J. C. RYLE

It is a grand thing to be driven to think; it is a grander thing to be driven to pray through having been made to think. What is faith, unless it is to believe what you do not see?

SAINT AUGUSTINE OF HIPPO

# A Family of Believers

God's family is like your own biological family. You're bound to get along better with some members than with others. When God paints a picture of unity among His people, it doesn't mean disagreements and misunderstandings disappear. It simply means that the faith you share will encourage you to work through any problems that arise. Together as God's family you can learn what love really looks like, encouraging one another toward growth while helping smooth out each other's rough edges.

## DAY 156

# Freer with Rules

Without rules, what sounds like freedom can be chaos. Take driving, for instance. You need a license to operate a motor vehicle because traffic flows "freer" when everyone knows, and follows, the rules. The same is true when living a life of faith. We are set free by salvation. . .but we are freer when we obey God. God's commandments help us build stronger relationships. We're freer to be ourselves, and love God and others well when we follow His rules.

# Worth Waiting For

The future isn't something that's waiting off in the distance. It's right here, right now. Every breath you take brings you into that future, one step at a time. And the future that awaits you is good. Faith changes the course of your future as surely as it changes the landscape of your heart. God is preparing a home for you that will never be torn down, a place where your questions will be answered and your longings, fulfilled.

## DAY 158

*Boldness*

*Having therefore, brethren, boldness to enter into the holiest by the blood of Jesus, by a new and living way, which he hath consecrated for us, through the veil, that is to say, his flesh; and having an high priest over the house of God; let us draw near with a true heart in full assurance of faith, having our hearts sprinkled from an evil conscience, and our bodies washed with pure water. Let us hold fast the profession of our faith without wavering; (for he is faithful that promised).*

HEBREWS 10:19–23 KJV

DAY 159

## Let It Flow

You can't be a good woman without doing good things. That isn't a rule. It's more of a reminder. Goodness flows naturally from a faith-filled heart. As you grow in your faith, you're changed from the inside out. You become more loving as you draw closer to our loving God. Your once prideful, self-centered heart begins to put others' needs before your own. Say yes to letting goodness flow freely from your life into the lives of others.

## DAY 160

## Faith Map

If you're navigating a road trip, just owning a map isn't going to get you to your destination. You need to compare where you are on the map with where you want to go, follow road signs, and evaluate your progress. God's Spirit works in much the same way. Each morning ask Him to help you head in the right direction. Then, throughout the day, evaluate where you are with where, and who, you believe God wants you to be.

## DAY 161

# Lend a Helping Hand

*Those of us who are strong and able in the faith need to step in and lend a hand to those who falter, and not just do what is most convenient for us. Strength is for service, not status. Each one of us needs to look after the good of the people around us, asking ourselves, "How can I help?" That's exactly what Jesus did. He didn't make it easy for himself by avoiding people's troubles, but waded right in and helped out.*

ROMANS 15:1–3 MSG

DAY 162

## Track Record of Hope

What do you hope for? *Really* hope for? Perhaps it's security, significance, or a relationship that will never let you down. Hopes like these are fulfilled solely through faith. Read God's track record as recorded in the Bible. He keeps His promises in areas like these time and again. It's true that it takes faith to place your hope in someone you can't see. But you're building your own track record with God. Day by day, you'll discover more reasons to hope in Him.

## DAY 163

## Humble Reflection

A humble woman sees herself through God's eyes. She recognizes the unique strengths God has built into her character. She sees herself as a creative collage of personality traits, talents, and abilities. . .but she's also well aware of her weaknesses. She knows that without God, even her strengths would not be enough to catapult her into becoming the woman she wants to be. Look at yourself through God's eyes today. Who do you see?

## DAY 164

# *Diligence*

*But, beloved, we are persuaded better
things of you, and things that accompany
salvation, though we thus speak. For God
is not unrighteous to forget your work and
labour of love, which ye have shewed toward
his name, in that ye have ministered to the
saints, and do minister. And we desire that
every one of you do shew the same diligence
to the full assurance of hope unto the end:
that ye be not slothful, but followers
of them who through faith and
patience inherit the promises.*

HEBREWS 6:9–12 KJV

## DAY 165

# In the Wilderness

*Father, I read in Luke about John the Baptist's ministry. His exhortations were aimed at the "wilderness of men's souls." Today many claim the faith yet exist in a wasteland of sin. I see it all around me, and sometimes in my own heart too. Help me proclaim Your Word and love to anyone, anwhere. Deepen my faith. Expose sin in my life. I want to live a life dedicated to declaring the Good News that saves us from the wilderness! Amen.*

## Living by Faith

Before you could read, letters were meaningless squiggles on the page. But with practice, and a parent's or teacher's help, one day everything clicked. Squiggles transformed into words—and stories. God is like those letters. However, you can't master the art of living by faith simply by studying about God. You need to humbly admit your wrongs. Accept God's forgiveness. Pray daily for growth and guidance. Then you'll learn who God really is and understand your part in His story.

DAY 167

## Increase Our Faith!

And if he trespass against thee seven times in
a day, and seven times in a day turn again to
thee, saying, I repent; thou shalt forgive him.
And the apostles said unto the Lord, Increase
our faith. And the Lord said, If ye had faith as
a grain of mustard seed, ye might say unto
this sycamine tree, Be thou plucked up
by the root, and be thou planted in
the sea; and it should obey you.

LUKE 17:4–6 KJV

## Gracious Patience

We're thankful for God's patience with us. He consistently honors us with time to grow, room to fail, and an endless supply of mercy and love. But we aren't the only ones who benefit from His patience. He extends it to everyone, including those we feel are slow learners or those we consider hopeless cases. In God's eyes, and in God's timing, there's always hope. Ask God to help you extend to others what He so graciously extends to you.

## DAY 169

# *Faithful in Prayer*

How do you build a relationship with a friend? You spend time together. You talk about everything, openly sharing your hearts. Prayer is simply talking to your best Friend. True, it's harder to understand God's reply than it is to read a friend's text or pick up her phone message. But the more frequently you pray, the easier it is to recognize God's voice. So keep talking. God's listening. With time, you'll learn how to listen in return.

## DAY 170

*Given Life*

"I know your afflictions and your poverty—
yet you are rich! I know about the slander of
those who say they are Jews and are not, but
are a synagogue of Satan. Do not be afraid
of what you are about to suffer. I tell you, the
devil will put some of you in prison to test
you, and you will suffer persecution for ten
days. Be faithful, even to the point of death,
and I will give you life as your victor's crown."

REVELATION 2:9–10 NIV

DAY 171

## Priorities

Eating, sleeping, working, praying, paying bills, staying fit, spending time with those you love. . .there are so many different priorities that cry out for your time each day. If you're struggling to figure out how to balance them all, allow your faith to help put things in perspective. What's God's priority for you? That you live a life of love and integrity. Keep these two things in mind as you decide what to add, and remove, from your schedule today.

DAY 172

## Getting to Know Him

Faith is not a to-do list of assignments from God. It's an invitation to relationship. It's about getting to know who God is and who He created you to be by spending time in His Word. It's about resting in God's love and acceptance, not working harder to prove yourself worthy of His affection. If you're suffering from spiritual burnout, take time to simply relax in God's presence, enjoying His company the way He enjoys yours.

## DAY 173

# Now Found

You're lost at sea, drowning. There's no hope of saving yourself. Then, members of the Coast Guard appear. They pull you from the frigid water—no questions asked. They don't save you because of your impressive résumé or because you're such a kind person. They save you because you need saving. Jesus saved you because you took hold of His hand in faith when He offered to pull you from the waves. Without Him, you were lost. Now, you're found—saved and secure.

## DAY 174

### Let the Light In

"It's obvious, isn't it? The place where your
treasure is, is the place you will most want to
be, and end up being. Your eyes are windows
into your body. If you open your eyes wide
in wonder and belief, your body fills up with
light. If you live squinty-eyed in greed and
distrust, your body is a dank cellar. If you
pull the blinds on your windows,
what a dark life you will have!"

MATTHEW 6:21–23 MSG

## Faith into Action

The most important choice you'll ever make is whether to serve God or yourself. The good news is that by choosing to serve God, you wind up doing what's best for yourself as well. Caring for the body God's given you is one way of serving Him. That includes eating a healthy diet, exercising regularly, getting annual check-ups, and using your body in ways that honor God and others. It's just one more way of putting your faith into action.

## DAY 176

# Blossoming for God

As you grow close to God, you blossom spiritually. But this is one flower that will never fade or fall. Your body will age, but spiritually, you'll continue to grow stronger and more beautiful. The more time you spend with God, the more your character will begin to resemble His—and the more humble you'll find yourself in His presence. This is exactly the kind of woman God's looking for to do wonderful things in this world.

DAY 177

# Help My Unbelief!

And [Jesus] asked [the child's] father,
How long is it ago since this came unto him?
And he said, Of a child. And ofttimes it hath
cast him into the fire, and into the waters,
to destroy him: but if thou canst do any
thing, have compassion on us, and help us.
Jesus said unto him, If thou canst believe,
all things are possible to him that believeth.
And straightway the father of the child
cried out, and said with tears, Lord,
I believe; help thou mine unbelief.

MARK 9:21–24 KJV

# Eyes of Faith

Faith gives you new eyes, along with a new heart. As you look more consistently in God's direction, you become aware of things you never noticed before. . .the miraculous detail of God's creation, the countless gifts He gives each day, His answers to prayer, and His persistence in bringing something positive out of even the most negative circumstances. It's good to notice God at work. It's even better to say "thank You" when you do. What will you thank Him for today?

## DAY 179
### *Faithful Work*

*Lord, when I'm broken, You heal my wounds. When I am anxious, You calm my fears. When I wander, You draw me close to You. When I am lost, You make my way clear. When I am tired, You provide the rest my soul craves. Lord, You restore me when I come to You, by renewing my spirit and deepening my faith. Thank You for Your faithful work in my life. I worship Your majesty and power. Amen.*

## Go to Jesus

There is not a thought, a feeling, or a circumstance, with which you may not go and tell Jesus. There is nothing that you may not in the confidence of love, and in the simplicity of faith, tell Jesus.

OCTAVIUS WINSLOW

The man is perfect in faith who can come to God in the utter dearth of his feelings and desires, without a glow or an inspiration, with the weight of low thoughts, failures, neglects, and wandering forgetfulness, and say to Him, "Thou art my refuge."

GEORGE MACDONALD

DAY 181

## Do You Believe?

*Nathanael answered and saith unto him,
Rabbi, thou art the Son of God; thou art
the King of Israel. Jesus answered and said
unto him, Because I said unto thee, I saw
thee under the fig tree, believest thou?
thou shalt see greater things than these.
And he saith unto him, Verily, verily, I say
unto you, Hereafter ye shall see heaven
open, and the angels of God ascending
and descending upon the Son of man.*

JOHN 1:49–51 KJV

## DAY 182

### Keep Watching

If asked about your favorite pastime, chances are "waiting" will never make it to the top of your list. But waiting is not wasted time. It's growing time. It's time to stay alert, to keep watch, to strengthen you faith, to look for signs that God's on the move. You're like a watchman waiting for sunrise. You know it's coming. You see signs of its arrival before it's fully dawn. Whatever you're waiting on God for today, keep watching. He's on the way.

# Circle of Love

When you worship God, you look at Him. You focus on who He is and what He's done. The thanks, the prayers, the songs, and the actions that flow out of this time are all different forms of worshipping the One who's given you life— and so much more. When you focus on God, you see more clearly how closely He's focusing on you. Worship weaves a reciprocal circle of love, one that will never end.

## DAY 184

## The Three-Legged Race

Marriage is like a three-legged race. Unless you work together, you're likely to take a few tumbles before crossing the finish line. Think of faith as the rope that holds you close. It binds you together, whether you're currently in sync or not. As you communicate with God, and each other, God will help set your pace and direct your course. The more you allow God to humble your pride, the easier your relational race will be.

## Promises, Promises

It's been said that death and taxes are the only things we can be certain of in our lives. The Bible tells us that faith brings its own gift of certainty. Because of God's promises, and His faithfulness in keeping them in the past, we have the assurance that He'll come through for us in the future. He's promised we're loved, forgiven, cared for, and destined for heaven. Rest in the fact that what God promises, He delivers.

## Bread of Life

*Then Jesus declared, "I am the bread of life. Whoever comes to me will never go hungry, and whoever believes in me will never be thirsty. But as I told you, you have seen me and still you do not believe. All those the Father gives me will come to me, and whoever comes to me I will never drive away. . . . I shall lose none of all those he has given me, but raise them up at the last day.*

JOHN 6:35–37, 39 NIV

# Faithful Choices

Free will is a wonderful gift. It allows you to have a say in the storyline of your life. But there are consequences tied to every decision you make, big or small. That's why making wise decisions is so important. The more you allow your faith to influence the decisions you make, the closer you'll be to living the life God desires for you. Invite God into your decision process. Let your "yes" or "no" be preceded by "amen."

# The Hand of Faith

As you read the Bible, do you sometimes wonder, as Jesus' disciples did, why Jesus used parables so often during His ministry on earth? Jesus' parables were words of truth hidden under an imaginary net. Only with the hand of faith could His followers lift a corner of the net and view the truth. Yet to those who He knew would respond, to those who had faith, He provided plain words. How open have you been to God's Word?

DAY 189

## *Where Your Treasure Is. . .*

". . .there will your heart be also" (Matthew 6:21 KJV). What does your heart long for? If you look at the root of every deep desire, you'll find something only God can fill. Love, security, comfort, significance, joy. . .trying to satisfy these desires apart from God can only yield limited success. God is the only one whose love for you will never waver. You're His treasure and His desire is to spend eternity with you. As your faith grows, so will your desire to treasure Him in return.

## DAY 190

*First Eyewitness*

*Now when Jesus was risen early the first day of the week, he appeared first to Mary Magdalene, out of whom he had cast seven devils. And she went and told them that had been with him, as they mourned and wept. And they, when they had heard that he was alive, and had been seen of her, believed not. . . . Afterward he appeared unto the eleven as they sat at meat, and upbraided them with their unbelief and hardness of heart.*

MARK 16:9–11, 14 KJV

## DAY 191

### Freedom's Price Tag

Imagine being locked in prison for years. You're guilty, hopeless, helpless. Then, a beloved friend volunteers to take your place. You're set free as another takes your punishment as their own. How much do you value the cost of your freedom? In essence, this is what Christ did for you. When you place your faith in Him, you're handed the key to freedom. Honor Jesus' gift by living a life worthy of such sacrifice.

## DAY 192

### The Waiting Game?

One of the biggest tests of faith? Waiting. You've prayed; you're poised on the edge of your seat waiting for an answer. . .but God remains silent. Will you lose faith? In times of waiting, remember that God won't withhold from you just to be cruel or make a point, but He does see the big picture, and He knows the right when, where, and how. So don't get anxious, just wait. You will see what God has promised you—all in due time.

# DAY 193

## Better Than Sight

Dark as my path may seem to others, I carry a magic light in my heart. Faith, the spiritual strong searchlight, illumines the way, and although sinister doubts lurk in the shadow, I walk unafraid toward the enchanted wood where the foliage is always green, where joy abides. . .in the presence of the Lord.

HELEN KELLER

Your faith would lose its glory if it rested on anything discernible by the carnal eye. Faith takes God without any ifs. If God says anything, faith says, "I believe it"; faith says, "Amen" to it.

D. L. MOODY

## Grow in Wisdom

The Holy Spirit dwells within you, ready to give you the wisdom you need to make good choices for your life. If you're listening, you will hear Him; but He is a gentleman. He won't shout or force you to hear what He has to say. As you seek Him through scripture and prayer, little by little your ears are tuned to His voice. The more you trust His lead, the more you will grow in wisdom.

## DAY 195

*Love*

*Whosoever shall confess that Jesus is the Son of God, God dwelleth in him, and he in God. And we have known and believed the love that God hath to us. God is love; and he that dwelleth in love dwelleth in God, and God in him. Herein is our love made perfect, that we may have boldness in the day of judgment: because as he is, so are we in this world.*

1 John 4:15–17 KJV

DAY 196

## Above All

Talking about faith can get tricky at times. What you believe, and how faith plays a part in your everyday life, may differ from those around you—even from those who attend the same church. Faith is important. But so is love and acceptance. God wholeheartedly accepts each and every one of His children and asks that we do the same. Listen in love. Learning to accept others the way Jesus did is more important than always seeing eye-to-eye.

# A Secret Worth Sharing

When it comes to family recipes, women often remain mum on the secret ingredient that makes their great-grandmother's pot roast, pound cake, or pickled beets stand out from the rest. You have a secret ingredient in your life that assures your future will turn out perfectly. But this secret—that once you put your faith in Jesus, you are assured of spending eternity with Him—is meant for sharing. Pass it on—and you'll be blessing future generations!

DAY 198

## *All That Matters*

And if you try to please God by obeying the Law, you have cut yourself off from Christ and his wonderful kindness. But the Spirit makes us sure that God will accept us because of our faith in Christ. If you are a follower of Christ Jesus, it makes no difference whether you are circumcised or not. All that matters is your faith that makes you love others. You were doing so well until someone made you turn from the truth.

GALATIANS 5:4–7 CEV

## Life of Faith

Jesus, You often used parables in Your earthly ministry—using a physical reality to get across a spiritual truth. But the disciples sometimes missed the point. They were faithful men, and yet they could not always comprehend Your divine ways. Please expand the little faith I have and provide me with real comprehension. I want to soak up all that I can from Your Word so that I may live well this life of faith. Amen.

## DAY 200

### Into Practice

What you do with God's words is ultimately what you decide to do with God. If you read the Bible for inspiration, without application, your faith will never be more than a heartwarming pastime. While it's true the Bible can be a source of comfort, it's also a source of power and an instrument of change. Invite God's Spirit to sear the Bible's words into your heart. Then step out in faith and put what you've learned into practice.

DAY 201

*One Together*

Neither pray I for these alone, but for them also which shall believe on me through their word; that they all may be one; as thou, Father, art in me, and I in thee, that they also may be one in us: that the world may believe that thou hast sent me. And the glory which thou gavest me I have given them; that they may be one, even as we are one.

JOHN 17:20–22 KJV

## DAY 202
## *"Adieu!"*

Change is a combination of embracing and letting go. When you become a mom, you welcome new love and bid "adieu" to some former freedoms. When you put your faith in God, you embrace the guidance of God's Spirit and abandon your old, self-centered agenda. When times get tough, it's tempting to seek comfort by looking to the past. But life only moves in one direction. Forward. Only by letting go of yesterday can you welcome today's opportunities with open arms.

## Life Preserver

If you were shipwrecked, you'd cling to your life preserver in hope of rescue. Faith is your life preserver in this world. It keeps your head above water in life and carries you safely into God's arms after death. But it takes commitment to keep holding on tight. Emotions rise and fall. Circumstances ebb and flow. But God is committed to you. His love and faithfulness never fail. By holding tightly to your faith, you can weather any storm.

DAY 204

*Put to Shame*

*Whether of them twain did the will of his father? They say unto him, The first. Jesus saith unto them, Verily I say unto you, That the publicans and the harlots go into the kingdom of God before you. For John came unto you in the way of righteousness, and ye believed him not: but the publicans and the harlots believed him: and ye, when ye had seen it, repented not afterward, that ye might believe him.*

MATTHEW 21:31–32 KJV

## Better Than

There's a bumper sticker that claims THE ONE WHO DIES WITH THE MOST TOYS WINS. If God wrote a bumper sticker, it might read THE ONE WHO'S CONTENT WITH WHAT SHE HAS TRULY LIVES. As your desire for God grows, your longing for more "stuff" takes a distant backseat. That's because through faith you begin to understand how rich you truly are. God's gifts are better than anything this world has to offer—filling your heart, instead of just your home.

## Out of Your Hands

From the man you choose to marry to how you style your hair, decisions are part of your daily life. But that doesn't mean you're totally in control. Much of life is out of your hands and solely in God's. That's where faith provides a place of peace. Rest in the knowledge that God is working behind the scenes to bring about good in your life. The best decision you'll ever make is to trust in His love for you.

# Faith Made Perfect

*Yea, a man may say, Thou hast faith, and I have works: shew me thy faith without thy works, and I will shew thee my faith by my works. Thou believest that there is one God; thou doest well: the devils also believe, and tremble. But wilt thou know, O vain man, that faith without works is dead? Was not Abraham our father justified by works, when he had offered Isaac his son upon the altar? Seest thou how faith wrought with his works, and by works was faith made perfect?*

JAMES 2:18–22 KJV

## DAY 208

### Erased!

You wouldn't ask a gardener to trim your hair or a house painter to paint your nails. When you ask someone to do something, you ask only those who you believe can actually do what needs done. God can do anything that's in line with His will. If you pray without expecting God to answer, doubt is derailing your faith. Ask God to help you understand the "whys" behind your doubts. He can help you erase each one.

## Wait Expectantly

If you're expecting an important package, you're often on the lookout for the mail carrier. You peek out the window. Listen for footsteps. Check the mailbox. When you pray, are you on the lookout for God's answers? Not every answer will be delivered when, where, and how you expect. So keep your eyes open and your heart expectant. Allow your faith to sustain you so you don't miss out on the joy of catching a glimpse of God at work.

## DAY 210

### Believe in the Midst

Thank God then if you have been led by a rough road. It is this which has given you your experience of God's greatness and loving-kindness. It is faith that brings power, not merely praying and weeping and struggling, but believing, daring to believe the written Word with or without feeling.

CATHERINE BOOTH

When outward strength is broken, faith rests on the promises. In the midst of sorrow, faith draws the sting out of every trouble and takes out the bitterness from every affliction.

ROBERT CECIL

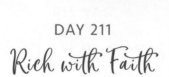

DAY 211

## Rich with Faith

*Listen, my dear brothers and sisters!
God chose the poor in the world to be rich
with faith and to receive the kingdom God
promised to those who love him. But you
show no respect to the poor. The rich are
always trying to control your lives. They are
the ones who take you to court. And they are
the ones who speak against Jesus, who owns
you. This royal law is found in the Scriptures:
"Love your neighbor as you love yourself."
If you obey this law, you are doing right.*

JAMES 2:5–8 NCV

## DAY 212

## *Anchor*

*When this life is uncertain, Lord, my soul clings to You. My future is secure because of my faith in the work Your Son did on the cross, dying for me. I look forward to the peace in spending eternity with You. Lord, I can't even imagine what You have in store for me in heaven. But as I anchor my thoughts on eternity, please keep me faithful to complete the duties You've called me to on earth. Amen.*

# Child of God

In the grind of daily life—from work to helping family to chores to volunteering in small ways—sometimes you wonder if what you do really matters. It does. God sees even the mundane tasks of the day done in faith. And He will not forget you. He will be your companion day after day. And He will reward you for your faithfulness. Labor on, child of God. Sleep well at night knowing that God is pleased with you.

DAY 214

## Jesus Saves

We can't save anyone. No one comes to faith in God because we do all the right things, say all the right words, or give them books by the best apologists. All those things may help of course, but no one comes to God because another has witnessed "perfectly." What does save people is God's grace. While our attempts drawing others to Christ may sputter, God's will is perfect—and He is faithful to save.

## DAY 215

### *Selected*

God picked you out as his from the very start.
Think of it: included in God's original plan
of salvation by the bond of faith in the living
truth. This is the life of the Spirit he invited
you to through the Message we delivered,
in which you get in on the glory of our
Master, Jesus Christ. So, friends, take a firm
stand, feet on the ground and head high.
Keep a tight grip on what you were taught.

2 THESSALONIANS 2:13–15 MSG

## DAY 216

### Forever Companion

Again and again the promise is woven throughout scripture: God will not leave you. He is by your side even when He feels far away. Do you believe that? Take each step, obey, and fear not. One day, one moment at a time is all He asks. When troubles comes, look to Him, plant your feet on His path, and dig in. Don't waver! He'll show the best way. He has already walked the path.

# Can't Have One without the Other

Faith and forgiveness are two sides of the same coin. You cannot hold on to one without embracing the other. If you believe Jesus loves you so much that He would pay the penalty for your sins with His own life, then you must also believe that He wouldn't hold those sins against you any longer. If you're feeling guilty, talk to God. Your feelings are not always truth tellers. God's forgiveness is what makes spending eternity with Him a true paradise.

## DAY 218

*Everlasting Fruit*

Pick up a banana at the supermarket, forget about it for a few days, and *voilà*! You wind up with a black, mushy mess. There's only one kind of fruit that doesn't spoil. That's spiritual fruit. Because of your faith in God, you can trust He's growing wholesome, everlasting fruit in you. You can nurture this fruit, helping it grow to maturity, by watering it frequently with God's words. Read the Bible. Then watch what God produces in your life.

## DAY 219

# The Breastplate of Faith

*For they that sleep sleep in the night;
and they that be drunken are drunken in
the night. But let us, who are of the day,
be sober, putting on the breastplate of faith
and love; and for an helmet, the hope of
salvation. For God hath not appointed us
to wrath, but to obtain salvation by our
Lord Jesus Christ, who died for us,
that, whether we wake or sleep,
we should live together with him.*

1 Thessalonians 5:7–10 kjv

# A Gentle Hand

From surgery to tole painting, it takes a gentle hand to accomplish a delicate task. But sometimes gentleness is viewed as a sign of weakness. Gentleness is not less powerful or effective than strength. It's strength released in a controlled, appropriate measure. When sharing your faith, gentleness shows you care for others the way God does. Jesus was never pushy. He simply told the truth. Then He allowed others the freedom to choose what to do with it.

## DAY 221
### Follow Behind

When following a trail, you're really following those who came before you. Physically, they're no longer present. But you can follow what they left behind. Maybe a cairn points you in the proper direction. Perhaps you walk a path flattened by previous footfalls. Keep your eyes on Jesus the way you follow a trail. Read what other followers left behind—the Bible. Watch for signs of God's work in the world. Then keep walking, leaving a "faith" trail others can follow.

## DAY 222

# In His Arms

Our bodies are miraculous works of art. But they don't last forever. When you're ill or in pain, God is near. As any parent who's ever loved a child knows, He aches with you, as well as for you. When the hope of healing seems distant, if you've run out of words to pray, picture yourself safe in His arms. Wait quietly, expectantly. Listen for His words of comfort. Rest in His promised peace. Hold on to Him for strength.

# DAY 223
## The Flip Side

Fear imprisons, faith liberates; fear paralyzes, faith empowers; fear disheartens, faith encourages; fear sickens, faith heals; fear makes useless, faith makes serviceable—and, most of all, fear puts hopelessness at the heart of life, while faith rejoices in its God.

HARRY EMERSON FOSDICK

A burden, even a small one, when carried alone and in isolation can destroy us, but a burden when carried as part of God's burden can lead us to new life. That is the great mystery of our faith.

HENRI NOUWEN

DAY 224

*Christ in Me*

"For through the law I died to the law so that
I might live for God. I have been crucified
with Christ and I no longer live, but Christ
lives in me. The life I now live in the body,
I live by faith in the Son of God, who loved
me and gave himself for me. I do not
set aside the grace of God, for if
righteousness could be gained through
the law, Christ died for nothing!"

GALATIANS 2:19–21 NIV

## DAY 225

*A Well of Joy*

In the Declaration of Independence, American citizens are guaranteed the right to the "pursuit of happiness." That's probably because happiness is something that must constantly be pursued. Even if you catch it, you can't hold on to it. Joy, on the other hand, is a gift of dependence. The more you depend on God, the deeper your well of joy. Ask God to show you how to draw on that reserve of joy, in any and every circumstance.

## DAY 226
# Children of God

*That was the true Light, which lighteth every man that cometh into the world. He was in the world, and the world was made by him, and the world knew him not. He came unto his own, and his own received him not. But as many as received him, to them gave he power to become the sons of God, even to them that believe on his name: which were born, not of blood, nor of the will of the flesh, nor of the will of man, but of God.*

JOHN 1:9–13 KJV

## Faithful Leadership

It's a myth that lemmings will follow each other off a cliff. The same can't be said for people. Some people do unthinkable things as the result of following a leader who isn't worthy of admiration or imitation. If God places you in a position of leadership, whether at home, at work, at church, or in the community, recognize it for the privilege it is. Ask God to make you a faithful leader and to help you love those you lead, guiding them with humility and wisdom.

## DAY 228
## Faith in Tomorrow

*Father, it's so easy to get bogged down
by the cares of this life. There are so many
hurting hearts, so many causes that need
our attention. There nevers seems to be
an end to misery and misfortune. But You
promise that all bad things come to an
end. There will be a day when You wipe
away every tear. Until then, Father,
give me contentment with the blessings
I have and faith in tomorrow. Amen.*

# Faith and Science

It takes faith, and science, to appreciate the wonders of nature. Science describes the improbability of generations of butterflies migrating thousands of miles to specific destinations they've never experienced firsthand or the impossibly delicate balance of our orbiting solar system. Faith assures us God not only understands miracles like these but set them in motion. Surely, a God who cares for the tiniest detail of nature, is aware—and at work—in every detail of your life.

## DAY 230

### Lean on Him

Jesus literally went through hell for you. He suffered the pain of rejection and betrayal. He endured physical agony. He gave His life out of love for you. When you face what seems unendurable, hold on to Jesus. Cry out to Him for help and hope. Pray throughout the day, picturing Him by your side, holding you up when your own strength fails. Express your love for Him by leaning on Him. He's near to help you persevere.

# DAY 231

## Toward Unconditional Love

What are your greatest accomplishments? Earning a degree? Landing a big account? Lovingly leading a toddler through the terrible twos? Whatever you've accomplished, hard work undoubtedly played a part in your success. The same goes for relationships. Going beyond superficiality toward unconditional love is hard work. It's a relational journey that takes patience, perseverance, forgiveness, humility, and sacrifice. It's a journey God willingly took to build a relationship with you. Now it's your turn to follow in His relational footsteps.

## DAY 232

# *Without Delay*

*I will stand at my watch and station myself on the ramparts; I will look to see what he will say to me, and what answer I am to give to this complaint. Then the LORD replied: ". . . the revelation awaits an appointed time; it speaks of the end and will not prove false. Though it linger, wait for it; it will certainly come and will not delay. See, the enemy is puffed up; his desires are not upright— but the righteous person will live by his faithfulness."*

HABAKKUK 2:1–4 NIV

## Always Right

Wearing white after Labor Day used to be considered taboo. But what was accepted as "right" in your mother's generation is not always considered "right" today. With God, the rules never change. What's right is always right. Living a righteous life means consistently choosing to do what's right in God's eyes. Doing what's right may not always be the popular choice, but it will always be the loving choice, the one God would make if He were in your shoes.

## DAY 234
### Under Control

Have you ever excused your own poor behavior by saying, "That's just the way I am"? God's Spirit tells a different story about who you are. Through faith, you have the ability to live a life characterized by discipline and self-control. But the choice to live that life is up to you. Consider the "character flaws" you see in your life. Ask God to help you get these areas under control, one thought, word, or action at a time.

## DAY 235

### Powerful Words

Research tells us women speak about twice as many words as men do each day. That gives us twice as many reasons to pay attention to what we say! It's easy to let whatever pops into our heads pop out of our mouths, but the Bible reminds us that our words have power. We're responsible for how we use that power. Will we hurt or heal? Build up or tear down? Allow faith to help you choose wisely.

## DAY 236

## Nothing Wavering

Knowing this, that the trying of your faith
worketh patience. But let patience have her
perfect work, that ye may be perfect and
entire, wanting nothing. If any of you lack
wisdom, let him ask of God, that giveth to all
men liberally, and upbraideth not; and it shall
be given him. But let him ask in faith, nothing
wavering. For he that wavereth is like a wave
of the sea driven with the wind and tossed.

JAMES 1:3–6 KJV

## Success

Faith's definition of success differs from that of the world. Whereas our culture applauds people of fame, wealth, and power, faith regards those who live their lives according to God's purpose as successful. Committing whatever you do to God isn't asking Him to bless what you've already decided to do. It's inviting Him into the planning process. Make sure your dreams and goals are in line with God's. Then get to work—leaving the end result in His hands.

## DAY 238
### The Little Things

If you lean against a wall, you have faith in its integrity. You trust it won't crumble and leave you in a heap on the floor. If you trust God, you'll lean on Him. This is more than saying, "I believe." This is living what you believe. You may not always understand the "whys" behind God's ways, but the more you risk trusting Him with the little things, the more confident you'll be entrusting Him with the big ones.

DAY 239

## Active Faith

God. . .cannot believe for us. Faith is a gift of God. . .but whether or not we shall act upon that faith lies altogether within our own power. We may or we may not, as we choose.

A. W. TOZER

Do not rejoice in earthly reality, rejoice in Christ, rejoice in His word, rejoice in His law. . . . There will be peace and tranquility in the Christian heart; but only as long as our faith is watchful; if, however, our faith sleeps, we are in danger.

SAINT AUGUSTINE OF HIPPO

## DAY 240

# Good Things

God our Savior showed us how good and kind he is. He saved us because of his mercy, and not because of any good things that we have done. . . . Jesus treated us much better than we deserve. He made us acceptable to God and gave us the hope of eternal life. This message is certainly true. These teachings are useful and helpful for everyone. I want you to insist that the people follow them, so that all who have faith in God will be sure to do good deeds.

TITUS 3:4–5, 7–8 CEV

# Put Wisdom to Work

Wisdom not only knows the right thing to do, she knows the right time and place to do it. As you grow in your faith, you can't help but grow in this kind of wisdom. That's what happens when you spend time with an all-wise God. His character rubs off on you. As you more clearly see others from God's perspective, you'll grow wiser in how you put your God-inspired love into action. Put your wisdom to work today.

## DAY 242

# Never Forsaken

*Father, this crazy, out-of-control world seems to be getting worse all the time. We are pressed in with problems, crime, uncertainty, and fear on every side. You promised You would never leave or forsake us. I know You take each of us by the hand each day, gently leading us through the good times and the bad. May I never doubt your faithfulness, which you have shown time and again. I trust anew in Your love today. Amen.*

## Reach Out

In the beginning of the Bible, God says it isn't good for people to be alone. Then He introduces Adam to Eve. The rest is history. Family is God's idea—and it's a good one. Whether it's your own family, your brothers and sisters in faith, or a time-tested circle of familial friends, don't wait for others to reach out to you when you're feeling lonely. Make the first move. Reach out in faith. True love both gives and receives.

# DAY 244

## *Without Signs*

When he heard that Jesus was come out
of Judaea into Galilee, he went unto him,
and besought him that he would come down,
and heal his son: for he was at the point of
death. Then said Jesus unto him, Except ye
see signs and wonders, ye will not believe.
The nobleman saith unto him, Sir, come
down ere my child die. Jesus saith unto him,
Go thy way; thy son liveth. And the man
believed the word that Jesus had spoken
unto him, and he went his way.

JOHN 4:47–50 KJV

# DAY 245

## Faith in God

Ultimately, it's not what you do, but what you believe that's rewarded by God. You can fill your life with good deeds, even to the point of sacrificing your life. But if you're faith is in your own strength, abilities, or goodness—instead of God—your full reward will be the praise of those around you. However, if you're motivated by faith, the only reward you'll desire is pleasing God. Having faith in God truly is its own reward.

## Everywhere You Look

God's story is written in more places than the Bible. It's written in the glory of the setting sun, the faithfulness of the ocean tides, the symphony of a thunderstorm, and the detail of a dragonfly's wing. It's written in every cell of you. Take time to "read" more about who God is as described through His creation. Contemplate His organizational skills, creative genius, and love of diversity. Consider nature God's written invitation to worship and wonder.

# Perfectly Trustworthy

God's faithfulness to you never falters. It began before you were born and will last far beyond the day you die. Nothing you do, or don't do, can adversely affect His love and devotion. This kind of faithfulness can only come from God. Those who love you may promise they'll never let you down, but they're fallible. Just like you. Only God is perfect—and perfectly trustworthy. What He says, He does. Today, tomorrow, always.

## DAY 248

*Word of God*

*As ye know how we exhorted and comforted and charged every one of you, as a father doth his children, that ye would walk worthy of God, who hath called you unto his kingdom and glory. For this cause also thank we God without ceasing, because, when ye received the word of God which ye heard of us, ye received it not as the word of men, but as it is in truth, the word of God, which effectually worketh also in you that believe.*

1 THESSALONIANS 2:11–13 KJV

## DAY 249
# Walk of Faith

Every walk you take is a series of steps that moves you forward. Each day you live is like a single step, moving you closer to—or farther away—from God. That's why it's good to get your bearings each morning. Through reading the Bible and spending time with God in prayer, you'll know which direction to take as you continue your walk of faith. Day by day, God will guide you straight into His arms.

# Be Faithful in Respect

As a child, chances are you were taught to respect authority. Parents, teachers, police officers, the elderly—people whose relationship, experience, or profession put them in a position of influence over your life—were deemed worthy of honor and obedience. Now, as a child of faith, you've accepted God as the ultimate authority figure over you. Don't let that title scare you. God's love tempers the power of His position. Respecting Him is just one more way of worshipping Him.

DAY 251

## Why Reason?

Faith is for that which lies on the other side of reason. Faith is what makes life bearable, with all its tragedies and ambiguities and sudden, startling joys.

MADELEINE L'ENGLE

Read the Word, and it will be much for your comfort. Search it and you will grow strong in the Lord and in the power of His might. Faith will lead you where you cannot walk. Reason has never been a mountain climber.

E. W. KENYON

## DAY 252
## Bright Future Ahead

Leap of faith. Have you ever thought about that expression? Faith sometimes means taking leaps. . .stepping out of your comfort zone toward a future you may just see a glimmer of right now. The road ahead may not be easy, but it will be the greatest adventure, the greatest race you've ever attempted. And best of all, the destination is certain. Throw yourself unreservedly into the work that God has called you to. Take hold of your future with both hands.

DAY 253

## Inner Strength

When you invite God to fill your heart and life, you are strengthened from within. His strength literally becomes your strength, and He can use even your weaknesses for His glory. You are empowered to do, to stand, to fight, to conquer. . . If Christ is there, you don't need to reach outside yourself for strength. Reach inside and find all you need. Grab hold of your faith, and trust God to uphold you.

## DAY 254

### Reconciled

*Once you were alienated from God and were
enemies in your minds because of your evil
behavior. But now he has reconciled you
by Christ's physical body through death to
present you holy in his sight, without blemish
and free from accusation—if you continue in
your faith, established and firm, and do not
move from the hope held out in the gospel.
This is the gospel that you heard and
that has been proclaimed to every
creature under heaven.*

Colossians 1:21–23 niv

DAY 255

## Holy Armor

A Roman soldier's belt was more than a fashion accessory. It held all of his offensive weapons. A soldier's defensive gear included a helmet, breastplate, and shield—his armor. As a woman of faith, God is your armor. When you're under attack, God not only offers you protection, He promises you justice. Secure your life with God's truth. Then rest in the fact that He's working behind the scenes, always doing what is right and just.

## DAY 256

# Doubting Thomas

And after eight days again his disciples were
within, and Thomas with them: then came
Jesus, the doors being shut, and stood in
the midst, and said, Peace be unto you.
Then saith he to Thomas, Reach hither thy
finger, and behold my hands; and reach
hither thy hand, and thrust it into my side:
and be not faithless, but believing.
And Thomas answered and said
unto him, My LORD and my God.

JOHN 20:26–28 KJV

## DAY 257

### True Potential

Your life has incredible potential. It's filled with opportunities to love, laugh, learn, and make a positive difference in this world. Faith turns every opportunity into an invitation: Will you choose to live this moment in a way that honors God? What you do with your life matters. But, ultimately, who you become is more important than what you accomplish. As your faith grows, your heart more resembles God's own. That's when you recognize where your true potential lies.

## DAY 258

# Saved by Faith

You were saved by faith in God, who treats
us much better than we deserve. This is
God's gift to you, and not anything you have
done on your own. It isn't something you
have earned, so there is nothing you can
brag about. God planned for us to do good
things and to live as he has always wanted
us to live. That's why he sent Christ
to make us what we are.

EPHESIANS 2:8–10 CEV

## DAY 259

### Peace Agreement

When world leaders sign a peace treaty, they pledge to keep the terms of an agreement. They aren't agreeing to like it—or each other. When you put your faith in Christ's sacrifice on your behalf, you make peace with God. God pledges to forgive your past grievances and even future mistakes. But the peace between you and God is more than an agreement. It's the rebirth of a relationship. This peace is permanent, based on unconditional love, not legality.

# The Source of All Good Things

*Dear Father, may my words today show that
I recognize You as the source of all good
things. You know what I need, and You've
promised in Your Word to supply everything
I need. May I have faith in Your provision.
May my prayer reflect the apostle Paul in
saying, "I have learned the secret of being
content in any and every situation, whether
well fed or hungry, whether living in plenty
or in want" (Philippians 4:12 NIV). Amen.*

DAY 261

*Always Welcome*

Being in the presence of someone you've wronged isn't a comfortable place to be. Even after apologies have been offered and restitution made, a feeling of shame and unworthiness often lingers. This isn't the case in our relationship with God. When we set things straight through faith, all that lingers is God's love. Draw close to your heavenly Father in prayer. Never be afraid to enter His presence. You're always welcome, just as you are.

## DAY 262

# Delivered!

We do not know what we might have been if God's gracious protection had not been like a wall of fire around us, as it still is, for the Lord continues to deliver all those who put their trust in Him. Faith is a higher faculty than reason.

Philip James Bailey

God has delivered you; give Him your gratitude. He is delivering you; give Him your confidence. He will deliver you; give Him your joy. Faith is a strong power, mastering any difficulty in the strength of the Lord who made heaven and earth.

Corrie ten Boom

DAY 263

## Wanted: Renewal

Every woman has days when she's feeling weary. But sometimes, this feels more like the norm than just a down day. When this happens, welcome weariness as a messenger. It's a reminder you're in need of renewal. Get alone with God and ask, "Is there anything I need to change? What's out of my hands and in Yours alone?" Allow God to do His job. Then, through the strength God supplies, do what you can with what you have.

DAY 264

*Beliefs Deepened*

"I've told you this ahead of time, before it happens, so that when it does happen, the confirmation will deepen your belief in me. I'll not be talking with you much more like this because the chief of this godless world is about to attack. But don't worry—he has nothing on me, no claim on me. But so the world might know how thoroughly I love the Father, I am carrying out my Father's instructions right down to the last detail."

JOHN 14:29–31 MSG

# A Faithful Heart

Suppose you had a daughter who broke every rule you made. She jumped on the furniture, hit her little brother, and swiped money from your wallet. Every day. But every evening, she offered you her dessert, telling you how much she loved you. The next day it was disobedience as usual. Have you ever been that little girl in God's eyes? Making sacrifices in God's name is commendable. But first, do what God asks. The obedience of a faithful heart is God's favorite gift.

## Blessed Singleness

"God gives the gift of the single life to some" (1 Corinthians 7:7 MSG). Do you consider singleness a gift? Paul did. He was one of the most prolific writers in the New Testament. His letters to churches, like the one in Corinth, teach us a lot about what living a life of faith looks like. He believed that being single gave him more time and freedom to focus more fully on God. Ask God to reveal to you how being single at this time is a gift for you.

DAY 267

## Knowest Not?

Jesus answered and said unto him,
Art thou a master of Israel, and knowest not
these things? Verily, verily, I say unto thee,
We speak that we do know, and testify
that we have seen; and ye receive not our
witness. If I have told you earthly things,
and ye believe not, how shall ye believe,
if I tell you of heavenly things? . . .
Even so must the Son of man be lifted
up: that whosoever believeth in him
should not perish, but have eternal life.

JOHN 3:10–12, 14–15 KJV

## DAY 268

## Cultivate Faith

Only God can make a seed grow. But you can make conditions favorable to help that seed mature and bear fruit. The same is true with faith. Cultivate the seed of faith God's planted in you through obedience. When God reveals a weed budding in your character, pull it up by the roots. A fresh sprout of love? Water it regularly with kindness and sacrifice. Tend to your spiritual growth each day, and beautiful things will begin to take root.

## A Cheerful Giver

"God loves a cheerful giver" (2 Corinthians 9:7 NIV). Lord, I know Your heart when it comes to sharing my time and resources with others. But sometimes I struggle with uncertainty and selfishness. Guide me as I choose among many worthy causes; make me conscious of the blessings You have given me. Help me to be a cheerful giver so that I reflect Your love for me and the overwhelming grace you bestow each day. Amen.

## DAY 270

# *Separated by Nothing*

*Can anything separate us from the love
Christ has for us? . . . But in all these things
we are completely victorious through God
who showed his love for us. Yes, I am sure
that neither death, nor life, nor angels,
nor ruling spirits, nothing now, nothing in
the future, no powers, nothing above us,
nothing below us, nor anything else in
the whole world will ever be able to
separate us from the love of God
that is in Christ Jesus our Lord.*

ROMANS 8:35, 37–39 NCV

## DAY 271

### Change of Mind

Living a life that pleases God is more than doing the right thing. It's also thinking the right thing. That's because faith isn't about appearances. It's about reality. It's about all of you: body, mind, and spirit. This transformation doesn't happen overnight. But the more time you spend with God, the more aware you'll become of random thoughts that don't line up with your faith. Take those thoughts to God. Ask Him to help change your mind, for good.

DAY 272

*God's Time*

God is the master of perfect timing because He can see straight across the grand scheme of history. He can tell if what you're waiting for today would be even better if it was received tomorrow—or years down the road. As you grow in your faith, you'll grow to trust God's timing more and more. It will take time—God's time. But expect Him to surprise you with the perfect harvest always delivered at exactly the right time.

## Measured Efforts

Faith helps you focus on what's most important in life—and in work. But when you're working hard, it can be frustrating to be around people who are not. Instead of taking them to task, take them to God in prayer. Ask for wisdom in knowing what to do or say, or if you should take any action at all. Measure your own efforts against what God's asked you to do, instead of the efforts of those around you.

## DAY 274

# Such Great Faith

*The centurion replied, "Lord, I do not deserve to have you come under my roof. But just say the word, and my servant will be healed. For I myself am a man under authority, with soldiers under me. I tell this one, 'Go,' and he goes. . . ." When Jesus heard this, he was amazed and said to those following him, "Truly I tell you, I have not found anyone in Israel with such great faith. . . . Go! Let it be done just as you believed it would."*

Matthew 8:8–10, 13 niv

## Focus on You

Some wives are more precious than royal jewels. Others are royal pains. If you're married, how does your husband see you? As you grow in your faith, you may notice how everyone around you could use the lessons you're learning. But God asks you to be responsible only for your own growth. Focus on loving your spouse by praying for him, helping him, and encouraging him. Be the spouse you'd like to be married to and let God handle the rest.

DAY 276

*He Came to Save*

*For God sent not his Son into the world
to condemn the world; but that the world
through him might be saved. He that
believeth on him is not condemned: but he
that believeth not is condemned already,
because he hath not believed in the name
of the only begotten Son of God. And this is
the condemnation, that light is come into the
world, and men loved darkness rather than
light, because their deeds were evil.*

John 3:17–19 KJV

## God's Presence

At times, God's presence is elusive. Although you believe in Him, you forget He's there. But He's like the air around you: invisible, yet essential to life. Remind yourself of God's presence each morning as soon as you awake. Breathe in and thank God for His gift of life. Then breathe out, asking Him to make you more aware of His hand at work in your life. Throughout the day, just breathe—drawing near to the One who gave you breath.

# A Harvest Ahead

"But the fruit of the Spirit is love, joy, peace, longsuffering, gentleness, goodness, faith"(Galatians 5:22 KJV). Fruit doesn't ripen through its own hard work. It doesn't will itself to grow juicier. Fruit just does what it was created to do. It grows into something beautiful and beneficial. God's Spirit is the only one who can bring this spiritual fruit to maturity in you. But you can provide the proper conditions to encourage growth. Have faith that God is at work. Put into practice what you learn. Then have patience. Harvesttime is coming!

# Simple

It is a masterpiece of the devil to make us believe that children cannot understand religion. Would Christ have made a child the standard of faith if He had known that it was not capable of understanding His words?

D. L. Moody

The Christian faith engages the profoundest problems the human mind can entertain and solves them completely and simply by pointing to the Lamb of God.

A. W. Tozer

DAY 280

*Faith Reboot*

If your computer has a glitch, it's helpful to refresh the page or reboot the whole program by pushing RESTART. God helps us refresh, reboot, and restart by renewing us through His Spirit. When you're in need of refreshment— even if you've already spent time with God that day, reading the Bible, singing His praises, or praying—take time to sit quietly in God's presence. Push RESTART. Wait patiently, and expectantly, for a word from the One you love.

## Truth Revealed

*All of our praise rises to the One who is strong enough to make you strong, exactly as preached in Jesus Christ, precisely as revealed in the mystery kept secret for so long but now an open book through the prophetic Scriptures. All the nations of the world can now know the truth and be brought into obedient belief, carrying out the orders of God, who got all this started, down to the very last letter.*

ROMANS 16:25–26 MSG

## DAY 282

*Creation Speaks*

Our God cares about details. You see it throughout His creation. . .in the beauty of the smallest flower, the intricacy of tiny bugs. When you wonder if God is interested in the details of your life, consider the evidence demonstrated in nature. He cares about everything—no matter how inconsequential. The God who lovingly created and sustains even the smallest of this world's inhabitants cares about you—whom He has made "a little lower than the angels" (Psalm 8:5 NIV).

## DAY 283

# Rest Easy

If you've ever struggled with insomnia, you know how frustrating the endless tossing and turning can be. If you are a parent, you know how worries and problems can keep you from the rest you desperately need. As you fall asleep, think of just how much God loves you. Build your faith by recalling all He has done for you. Count your blessings instead of sheep; then sleep peacefully in your heavenly Father's protective arms.

## DAY 284

### Truly Successful

True success comes when you're willing to say, "It's not about me and all about You, Lord." Then He is free to take you to a level that you can only achieve with His strength and power propelling you. Letting God take control takes faith. Most of us are used to ordering our priorities and using our power to achieve our goals. But God's priorities are always best; and His power will always outlast ours. True success comes only through Him.

## DAY 285

## Heaven Awaits

*Let not your heart be troubled: ye believe in God, believe also in me. In my Father's house are many mansions: if it were not so, I would have told you. I go to prepare a place for you. And if I go and prepare a place for you, I will come again, and receive you unto myself; that where I am, there ye may be also. And whither I go ye know, and the way ye know.*

John 14:1–4 KJV

# One (Courageous) Step at a Time

In Jesus' day, women had fewer opportunities to stretch their wings creatively and professionally than they do today. That didn't stop them from holding tightly to God's promises and stepping out to act on what they believed. You can follow in their courageous footsteps. Whatever you believe God wants you to do, big or small, don't hold back. Today, take at least one step toward your goal. With God's help, you'll accomplish everything He's set out for you to do.

DAY 287

## Faith = Balance

Women are notorious for having moods that shift at the slightest provocation. We may blame it on hormones, stress, or the demands of those around us. Regardless of what pushes our mood swings to an all-time high, the truth is we all need an attitude adjustment now and then. Faith provides exactly what we require. As we turn to God in prayer, His Spirit makes us more like Him. He balances our lives, and emotions, with His power and perspective.

## Faithful Commitment

*Lord, how grateful I am that Your Holy Spirit worked in the lives of Your apostles, molding them into strong men of faith. They left everything—jobs, family, resources—behind and devoted their lives to proclaiming the good news of salvation. Help me become unselfish with my time so that many more will hear the Gospel. May I devote my everything to fulfill Your will. May my faith become as strong as theirs. Amen.*

## DAY 289

# Have Faith

But without faith no one can please God.
We must believe that God is real and that
he rewards everyone who searches for
him. . . . Even when Sarah was too old to
have children, she had faith that God would
do what he had promised, and she had a son.
Her husband Abraham was almost dead,
but he became the ancestor of many
people. In fact, there are as many of
them as there are stars in the sky or
grains of sand along the beach.

HEBREWS 11:6, 11–12 CEV

## DAY 290

### Burden Bearer

It's important for us women to do some heavy lifting as we age. Weight-bearing exercise helps keep our bones strong and our muscles toned. But bearing mental and emotional weight is another story. These don't build us up. They break us down. Allow faith to become your personal trainer when it comes to what's weighing heavily on your mind and heart. God knows how much weight you can bear. Invite Him to carry what you cannot.

## DAY 291

*A True Tale*

"Tell me a story. . . ." If you're a mom, you've probably heard those words time and time again. But have you ever told your children stories about your faith? How you came to believe in God and how He's been faithful to you in the past are a part of your spiritual family history. The next time a child asks for a story, tell a true tale of wonder and adventure. Tell a tale about God and His love.

# DAY 292

## *Awed*

When the Bible talks about the "fear of God" it's more about awe than alarm. Through faith, we catch a glimpse of how powerful God really is and how small we are in comparison. Yet the depth of God's love for us rivals the enormity of His might. Regardless of the troubles that may surround you, or what you see on the evening news, you can be confident that God remains in charge, in control, and deeply in love.

## DAY 293

*Inheritance*

*In whom also we have obtained an inheritance, being predestinated according to the purpose of him who worketh all things after the counsel of his own will: that we should be to the praise of his glory, who first trusted in Christ. In whom ye also trusted, after that ye heard the word of truth, the gospel of your salvation: in whom also after that ye believed, ye were sealed with that holy Spirit of promise, which is the earnest of our inheritance until the redemption of the purchased possession, unto the praise of his glory.*

EPHESIANS 1:11–14 KJV

## DAY 294

## Faith-Filled Devotion

Our devotion to God leads us to be more devoted to others. That's because God's Spirit is at work in us, encouraging us to do what's right. When we keep our promises, weigh our words, and offer a helping hand with no expectation of reward, we are loving God by loving others. Our faith-filled devotion to God brings out the best in us, while at the same time blessing those around us.

## DAY 295
## *"Follow My Lead"*

The Bible's a pretty thick book. It looks like there's a lot to learn. But Jesus said that if we love God and others, we've fulfilled everything written there. How do we do that? Look to Jesus' own life as recorded in the Gospels. Jesus never treats people like an interruption or inconvenience. He listens, comforts, and cares. He spends time with His Father in prayer, regardless of His busy schedule. Jesus' example is one worth following.

DAY 296

## Faithful Examples

Reading how women have faced difficult circumstances, yet found peace, power, and purpose through faith can be a source of comfort. Whether the account is about Lazarus's sisters, Mary and Martha; the woman caught in adultery or the Samaritan at the well, these women all found comfort in Christ's words. In turn, we can be comforted by their experiences. Just as Christ changed their hearts and lives, His words and His love can do the same for us today.

## DAY 297

# Produced by Faith

*We always thank God for all of you and
continually mention you in our prayers.
We remember before our God and Father
your work produced by faith, your labor
prompted by love, and your endurance
inspired by hope in our Lord Jesus Christ.
For we know, brothers and sisters loved by
God, that he has chosen you, because our
gospel came to you not simply with words
but also with power, with the Holy
Spirit and deep conviction.*

1 Thessalonians 1:2–5 niv

## Friend or Foe?

Do you regard your emotions as friend or foe? Your answer may depend on how much they control your life. God created you as a woman, an emotional being. Your wide range of emotions—including empathy, anger, compassion, joy, sorrow, and fear—all help you assess situations and decide on appropriate action. But it takes God's wisdom to balance the power of your emotions. It takes faith to place your situation in God's hands. When emotions run high, ask God for control and clarity before you act.

### DAY 299

## Our Defense

If you've been hurt by someone you trusted, choose to release that person today. Let it go. God is your defender. He's got your back. Take refuge in Him. And remember, praising Him—even in the storm—will shift your focus back where it belongs. Have faith that the one who died to set us free, who loves us with an everlasting love, will defend those He paid a high price for. Praise the Lord! He is our defense!

DAY 300

## Once Begun

Grace be unto you, and peace, from God
our Father, and from the Lord Jesus Christ.
I thank my God upon every remembrance of
you, always in every prayer of mine for you all
making request with joy, for your fellowship
in the gospel from the first day until now;
being confident of this very thing, that he
which hath begun a good work in you will
perform it until the day of Jesus Christ.

PHILIPPIANS 1:2–6 KJV

## DAY 301

*Dollars*

A sense of entitlement comes with a paycheck. You earned it, so you get to choose how to spend it, right? But have you ever stopped to consider how the way God created you impacts your ability to earn a living? Take a moment right now to thank God for His part in your financial picture. Ask Him to give you wisdom, self-control, and a spirit of generosity as you choose how to use every dollar you receive.

DAY 302

*How Far*

Battles may be foreseen, and woe to the man who does not expect them, but the eye of faith perceives the crown of victory. Faith is not shelter against difficulties, but belief in the face of all contradictions.

PAUL TOURNIER

The greatest proof of Christianity for others is not how far a man can logically analyze his reasons for believing, but how far in practice he will stake his life on his belief.

T. S. ELIOT

## DAY 303

### Inside Job

Faith is the ultimate makeover. But it doesn't hide who you are with a lift or tuck here and a fresh coat of foundation there. This makeover isn't external. It's eternal. And it's totally an inside job. Jesus referred to it as being "born again." Those old habits, regrets, and mistakes are behind you. Your past is forgiven and your future empowered by God's Spirit working through you. Let go of yesterday and grab hold of God's promise for today!

## DAY 304

# Is Anything Impossible?

*Therefore Sarah laughed within herself,
saying, After I am waxed old shall I have
pleasure, my lord being old also? And the
LORD said unto Abraham, Wherefore did
Sarah laugh, saying, Shall I of a surety bear a
child, which am old? Is any thing too hard for
the LORD? At the time appointed I will return
unto thee, according to the time of life, and
Sarah shall have a son. Then Sarah denied,
saying, I laughed not; for she was afraid.*

GENESIS 18:12–15 KJV

## DAY 305

# Faith for Every Day

*Lord, Your Word is filled with the miraculous.
I read about healing, provision, rescue—
about Jesus meeting every need in every
situation for those who came to Him in faith.
I come to You today with needs of my own.
You know what situations I face, and You
are ever faithful. Thank You for always
going well beyond what I expect or
ask. Strengthen my faith to meet the
challenges that lie ahead. Amen.*

# DAY 306
## Godly Leaders

A good leader is a godly leader. She recognizes her strengths and uses them in a way that honors God and others. Most importantly, she recognizes her greatest asset is prayer. If you ask God for wisdom, He promises He'll give it to you. Whether you're leading executives in the boardroom or preschoolers through a lesson in sharing, ask God for the right words, right timing, and right attitude so you can wisely lead others in the right direction.

DAY 307

## His Unfailing Love

When you first chose to believe in God, His grace wiped away every past digression you'd ever made from the life He designed for you to lead. But His grace doesn't stop there. Every day, it's at work. You may be God's daughter, but you're still growing. There'll be times you'll stumble. Times you'll look to yourself first, instead of to God. God's grace continues to cleanse you and draw you closer to Him, reassuring you of His unfailing love.

## To Your Health

Prayer is God's spiritual healthcare plan. Modern medicine can do wonderful things to help a sick person get well. But God knows your body better than anyone. He designed it. He can heal it. Not every prayer for healing is answered in the way and time frame we hope for. Sometimes, emotional or spiritual healing takes place, while physical healing does not. God can raise us up in different ways. So call on Him. You never need an appointment.

## Blessed Is She

And it came to pass, that, when Elisabeth
heard the salutation of Mary, the babe
leaped in her womb; and Elisabeth was filled
with the Holy Ghost: and she spake out
with a loud voice, and said, Blessed art thou
among women, and blessed is the fruit of
thy womb. And whence is this to me,
that the mother of my Lord should come
to me? For, lo, as soon as the voice of
thy salutation sounded in mine ears,
the babe leaped in my womb for joy.
And blessed is she that believed.

LUKE 1:41–45 KJV

## DAY 310

# A Life of Integrity

One of the hardest places to consistently live out what you believe is in your own home. That's because those who know you best have seen you at your worst. Living a life of integrity 24-7 takes more than self-control. It takes a change of heart. Only God can transform a selfish, wayward ego into a woman worth emulating. Place your faith in God's power, put your pride on the line, and then fully live what you say you believe.

# Gentlewomen

Society honors a gentleman. By definition, he's someone who treats others with courtesy, thoughtfulness, and respect. In contrast, a gentlewoman is often pictured as a proverbial wallflower, soft-spoken, and easily pushed around. Gentleness is a characteristic of the heart—a trait God honors and exemplifies. You can be a spitfire with a voice like a foghorn who's not afraid to stand up for what's right and still exude gentleness. Allow God to help bring out the gentlewoman in you.

## DAY 312

# Half Baked?

There's nothing delicious, delightful, or desirable about a half-baked cake. You have to wait until it's finished baking, no matter how hungry you are or how tight your time constraints may be. Impatience pushes us to take shortcuts and settle for second best. It can also rob us of opportunities to grow in our faith. The next time you feel impatience rising up in you, ask God, "What would You like me to learn while I wait?"

## DAY 313

## Rescued

GOD is gracious—it is he who makes
things right, our most compassionate God.
GOD takes the side of the helpless; when I
was at the end of my rope, he saved me.
I said to myself, "Relax and rest. GOD
has showered you with blessings. Soul,
you've been rescued from death; Eye,
you've been rescued from tears; and you,
Foot, were kept from stumbling." I'm striding
in the presence of GOD, alive in the land
of the living! I stayed faithful, though
bedeviled, and despite a ton of bad luck.

PSALM 116:5–10 MSG

DAY 314

## Holy Power Source

What happens if your blow-dryer won't blow?
First, you check out the power source. Without
power, a blow-dryer may look useful, but it's
really nothing more than a plastic knickknack. It's
God's power working through you that allows you
to accomplish more than you can on your own.
Staying connected with God through prayer,
obedience, reading the Bible, and loving others
well will keep His power flowing freely into your
life—and out into the world.

# DAY 315

## Wiped Clean

Saying you're righteous is the same as saying you're blameless. And that's what God says about you. Once you put your faith and trust in Jesus, every trace of your past rebellion against God is wiped away. It's as though you lived Jesus' life, morally perfect and wholly good. What's more, this righteousness covers your future, as well as your past. Anytime you stumble, go straight to God. Confess what you've done. You can trust it's forgiven and forgotten.

## DAY 316
### A Favorite Lullaby

Sleep can be elusive, particularly during certain seasons of a woman's life. If 2 a.m. feedings, the throes of menopause, or simply mentally sorting through the demands of daily life are keeping you awake, set aside your frustration. Picture yourself pulling up the blanket of darkness, settling into the silence of night. Then turn your thoughts to God. Pour out your problems or lift up your praises. Ask God for refreshment and renewal. Allow God's voice to become your favorite lullaby.

DAY 317

## Faithful to the Faithful

You are good to me, LORD, because I do right,
and you reward me because I am innocent.
I do what you want and never turn to do evil.
I keep your laws in mind and never look away
from your teachings. I obey you completely
and guard against sin. You have been good
to me because I do right; you have rewarded
me for being innocent by your standards.
You are always loyal to your loyal people,
and you are faithful to the faithful.

PSALM 18:20–25 CEV

# DAY 318

## Answered Prayer

*And [Hannah] said, Oh my lord, as thy soul liveth, my lord, I am the woman that stood by thee here, praying unto the LORD. For this child I prayed; and the LORD hath given me my petition which I asked of him: therefore also I have lent him to the LORD; as long as he liveth he shall be lent to the LORD. And he worshipped the LORD there.*

1 SAMUEL 1:26–28 KJV

DAY 319

## Second Wind

When you're feeling worn out, it's hard to think about meeting anyone's needs other than your own. But sometimes that's exactly what God asks you to do. Perhaps it's your children who need your help in the middle of the night. Or maybe it's a stranger whose car has broken down by the side of the road. When God nudges you to respond, call on Him for strength. His Spirit will rouse your compassion, providing you with a second wind.

## DAY 320

# Prayer for Faith

*I am hurting, Lord. The waves are crashing on the shore, and I confess that I've not kept my eyes fastened on You. I struggle under my own might and only draw myself deeper into the troubles. Though I may not know the outcome of everything in my life, dear Father, I am renewing my faith in Your power and wisdom in my life. I know You will not let me go. How my heart rejoices that I can trust in You! Amen.*

DAY 321

## Out of My Hands

There is no calm deeper than that which succeeds a storm. Our confidence must not be in what we have done nor in what we have resolved to do, but entirely in what the Lord will do. Pure and simple, faith not lived every day is not faith, it is facade.

UNKNOWN

As your faith is strengthened you will find that there is no longer the need to have a sense of control, that things will flow as they will, and that you will flow with them, to your great delight and benefit.

EMMANUEL TENEY

## DAY 322

# *What Lies Ahead*

You confide in a friend because she's proven herself faithful over time. She won't lie. What she says she'll do, she does. You trust in her love, because you believe she has your best interests at heart. God is this kind of friend. It takes time to build your own track record of trust with Him. As you do, consider His faithfulness to those in the Bible. God's past faithfulness can help you trust Him for whatever lies ahead.

## DAY 323

## Deeply Rooted

*God is wonderful and glorious. I pray that his Spirit will make you become strong followers and that Christ will live in your hearts because of your faith. Stand firm and be deeply rooted in his love. I pray that you and all of God's people will understand what is called wide or long or high or deep. I want you to know all about Christ's love, although it is too wonderful to be measured. Then your lives will be filled with all that God is.*

Ephesians 3:16–19 cev

## DAY 324

### Every Piece

Your life is a bit like a jigsaw puzzle, made up of multiple pieces. Some pieces are things you do. Others are things you are, have been, or hope to become one day. Your physical body, your emotional makeup, and the unique way your brain works are all part of this puzzle. To fully trust in God, you need to place every piece in His hands. Only God has the power to put you together perfectly.

# DAY 325

## Sing a Song

One day, everyone will know that what you believe is absolutely true. Jesus, the focus of your faith, will be visible to all. Every created being will fall facedown in awe at the mere mention of His name. But you don't have to wait until then. Each new day delivers a fresh invitation to worship, countless more reasons to lift up your praise. Worship is a song that has no end. What verse will your life sing to Jesus today?

DAY 326

## Use Those Gifts!

You are unique. Your blend of experience, talents, and personality are gifts you can share with the world. But when you choose to put your faith in God, you also receive "spiritual" gifts. God gives you these abilities so you can help others see Him more clearly. By using gifts such as teaching, serving, or giving encouragement, you make faith visible. Ask God to help you understand, and use, the gifts He's so graciously given to you.

## DAY 327
# Faith by Itself

My brothers and sisters, if people say they have faith, but do nothing, their faith is worth nothing. Can faith like that save them? A brother or sister in Christ might need clothes or food. If you say to that person, "God be with you! I hope you stay warm and get plenty to eat," but you do not give what that person needs, your words are worth nothing. In the same way, faith by itself—that does nothing—is dead.

JAMES 2:14–17 NCV

## DAY 328

# A Time to Celebrate

When you work hard toward completing a goal, accomplishing what you've set out to do is something worth celebrating. When your accomplishment is fueled by faith, you can be certain you'll never celebrate alone. God sees the time, energy, and heart you put into your work. Better yet, He adds His own power to your efforts. This means that with God, you can accomplish things you could never do solely on your own. That's something truly worth celebrating—with God!

## DAY 329

# Drawn to Jesus

Even those who don't believe Jesus is God can agree that He was an extraordinary person. The way Jesus selflessly loved others, reaching out to people society cast aside, demonstrates an attitude of compassion, humility, and service. We're drawn to those who sincerely care for us. That's one reason why we're drawn toward Jesus. Believing in a God who believes in us doesn't feel risky. It feels like accepting a free invitation to be unconditionally loved.

## DAY 330

### Trivialities

Him that is weak in the faith receive ye, but not to doubtful disputations. For one believeth that he may eat all things: another, who is weak, eateth herbs. Let not him that eateth despise him that eateth not; and let not him which eateth not judge him that eateth: for God hath received him. Who art thou that judgest another man's servant? to his own master he standeth or falleth. Yea, he shall be holden up: for God is able to make him stand.

ROMANS 14:1–4 KJV

## DAY 331

### Faith First

If you're searching for a pair of shoes, you don't rely on a salesperson's description. You want to see them. Try them on. Walk around in them awhile. The same is true when it comes to trying on faith for size. We long to see the One we've chosen to place our faith in. But Jesus says believing without seeing holds its own special reward. Ask Jesus to help you better understand those blessings as you walk in faith today.

DAY 332

## Head-On

The Bible tells us faith is what moves mountains. Not personal ability. Not perseverance. Not even prayer. These can all play a part in facing a challenge that looks as immovable as a mountain. But it's faith in God's ability, not our own, that's the first step toward meeting a challenge head-on—then conquering it. Remind yourself of what's true about God's loving character and incomparable power. Then move toward the challenge, instead of away from it. God's in control.

## DAY 333

## Faith without Sight

Father, this world demands evidence.
"Seeing is believing" is the anthem of our
day. Sometimes I find myself falling in
line and doubting what I can't grasp.
Remind me, Lord, that my faith in You is
not based in my senses or my intellect but
in Your never-failing love, which saved my
soul and promises me unspeakable joy.
Remind me of Your words, "Blessed are
they that have not seen, and yet have
believed" (John 20:29 KJV). Amen.

## DAY 334

# For Our Good

And we know that all things work together
for good to them that love God, to them
who are the called according to his purpose.
For whom he did foreknow, he also did
predestinate to be conformed to the image
of his Son, that he might be the firstborn
among many brethren. Moreover whom
he did predestinate, them he also called:
and whom he called, them he also justified:
and whom he justified, them he also
glorified. What shall we then say
to these things? If God be for us,
who can be against us?

ROMANS 8:28–31 KJV

# Limitless God

There's only so much one person can do. There are limits to your strength, your time, and your capacity to love others well. When you reach the limit of your own abilities, a feeling of helplessness can set in. But being helpless isn't synonymous with being hopeless. God is near. He hears every prayer, every longing, and every sigh. His power, love, and time are limitless. Cry out in faith when you need the comfort of your Father's love.

## DAY 336

## Even More

A mother's love could be considered the epitome of compassion. Mothers selflessly carry a child within their own body for nine months, then nourish the newborn with their own milk. They comfort, wean, clean, and cuddle. And if the situation arose, most mothers would sacrifice their own lives to save the children they love. Yet God's compassion runs even deeper than a mother's love. His loving care is passionate, powerful, and permanent for those who put their faith in Him.

DAY 337

## Live Fully in Faith

Imagine standing before a holy, almighty, and perfect God and being judged for how you've lived your life. Every mistake, poor choice, and moment of rebellion would be exposed. Sounds downright terrifying, doesn't it? But through our faith in Jesus, we have nothing to fear. We stand faultless and forgiven. Through Christ, we can gather the courage to look at ourselves as we really are, faults and all, without shame. Being wholly loved gives us the courage to fully live.

## DAY 338

# He Knows Your Needs

*God gives such beauty to everything
that grows in the fields, even though it is
here today and thrown into a fire tomorrow.
He will surely do even more for you!
Why do you have such little faith?
Don't worry and ask yourselves, "Will we
have anything to eat? . . . Will we have any
clothes to wear?" Only people who don't
know God are always worrying about such
things. Your Father in heaven knows
that you need all of these. But more
than anything else, put God's work
first and do what he wants.*

MATTHEW 6:30–33 CEV

DAY 339

## Right Here, Right Now

It's fun daydreaming about places you'd like to visit, goals you'd like to accomplish, or who you hope to mature into—someday. But God's only given you one life. Chances are, you'll have more dreams than you'll have days. Instead of living for "someday," God challenges you to put your heart into today. Whether you're sunning on vacation or scrubbing the kitchen floor, the God of the universe is right here with you. That's something worth celebrating!

## DAY 340

## At Rest

Faith is the root of all blessings. Believe, and you shall be saved; believe, and your needs must be satisfied; believe, and you cannot but be comforted and happy.

JEREMY TAYLOR

Faith makes all things possible. Hope makes all things bright. Love makes all things easy. The thought of You stirs us so deeply that we cannot be content unless we praise You, because You have made us for Yourself and our hearts find no peace until they rest in You.

SAINT AUGUSTINE OF HIPPO

## No Doubting, Just Faith

Entrusting friends and family to God's care isn't always easy. One reason is that as women, we're born caretakers—and we doubt anyone can care for those we love as well as we do. Faith assures us that God is the only perfect caregiver. When we worry about someone, we're doubting God's love, power, and plan for that person's life. Bring every doubt and worry to God in prayer. Allow Him to transform your doubts into faith.

# DAY 342

## Mustard-Seed Faith

*Jesus rebuked the demon, and it came out of the boy, and he was healed at that moment. Then the disciples came to Jesus in private and asked, "Why couldn't we drive it out?" He replied, "Because you have so little faith. Truly I tell you, if you have faith as small as a mustard seed, you can say to this mountain, 'Move from here to there,' and it will move. Nothing will be impossible for you."*

MATTHEW 17:18–20 NIV

DAY 343

## Faith by Example

As a child, perhaps you played "school" before you ever attended class. If you had the coveted role of "teacher," you got to tell your friends what to do. As an adult, you're still playing the role of teacher, whether you're aware of it or not. When what you believe changes the way you live and love, others notice. Who knows? The most powerful lessons you ever teach may be those where you never say a word.

DAY 344

*Armored in Faith*

*Wherefore take unto you the whole armour
of God, that ye may be able to withstand in
the evil day, and having done all, to stand.
Stand therefore, having your loins girt about
with truth, and having on the breastplate of
righteousness; and your feet shod with
the preparation of the gospel of peace;
above all, taking the shield of faith,
wherewith ye shall be able to quench
all the fiery darts of the wicked.*

EPHESIANS 6:13–16 KJV

DAY 345

## Faith's Testing Ground

Your family's unique. You may be married, single, with kids or without. Parents, siblings, aunts, cousins. . .they're all part of the family God's placed you in. That family can be a testing ground for faith. That's because the more time you spend with people, the easier it is for them to rub you the wrong way—and vice versa. Consider what God wants to teach you through your family. Patience? Forgiveness? Grace? Don't put off until tomorrow what you could learn today.

## DAY 346

### Refuel Your Faith

After a long, frustrating day at work, whether we use our muscles or brains on the job, we all know what it is to be worn out. But we can wear out spiritually too. Our faith levels can deplete as we become consumed by the world's demands and lose our focus on the Lord. Jesus tells us to come to Him when weariness floods our souls. When we drink deeply at His well, the energy will begin to flow.

# Surrendered to His Care

Father, I marvel that You know me so well. You count the hairs on my head. You care about the pain I experience and the troublesome times that I face. When a sparrow falls, You care. How much, then, You must care for me. Only You have the power to override earthly impossibilities. I pray today that no matter what appears to be impossible in my life, I'll be able to surrender it to Your care and trust. Amen.

DAY 348

*God's Ways*

Plans go awry; life gets messy. When you're tempted to shout, "What are You up to, God?" remember that while men's ways are variable, God's ways are everlasting. Pray. Pray some more; then watch for God's leading. Keep the faith. Take up your own daily cross; it is the burden best suited for your shoulder and will prove most effective to make you perfect in every good word and work to the glory of God.

## DAY 349
## Faithful Ones

*Some women received their loved ones back from death. . . . The world did not deserve these good people, who had to wander in deserts and on mountains and had to live in caves and holes in the ground. All of them pleased God because of their faith! But still they died without being given what had been promised. This was because God had something better in store for us. And he did not want them to reach the goal of their faith without us.*

HEBREWS 11:35, 38–40 CEV

## Measure Up

When God created each of us, He wove together a wonderful person unlike any other. But at times it's tempting to gauge how well we're doing by using others as a measuring stick. Faith offers a different standard. The Bible encourages us to use our abilities in ways that honor God. Some abilities may take center stage, while others work quietly in the background. Just do what you can with what you have in ways that make God smile. No comparison necessary.

## DAY 351

# The One Thing

When you were little, what was the "one thing" you wanted? You knew you'd truly be happy, if only it were yours. Adults often feel the same way. If only we had more money, this "one thing" could be ours! But when we focus on our wants, we become a slave to those longings. There's only "one thing" that truly satisfies—having faith in the God who loves you enough to provide exactly what you need.

## DAY 352

# Big-Hearted Generosity

When you choose to follow Christ, your faith opens the floodgates of countless good gifts. You receive things like forgiveness, salvation, a future home in heaven, and God's own Spirit living inside you. God's generosity is incomparable. It can also be motivational. When someone is incredibly generous with you, it inspires you to share more generously with others. Whether it's your time, your finances, your home—or things like forgiveness, grace, or love—follow God's example. Be big-hearted and open-handed.

# DAY 353
## Faithful with Much

*The servant who had been given two thousand coins came in and said, "Sir, you gave me two thousand coins, and I have earned two thousand more." "Wonderful!" his master replied. "You are a good and faithful servant. . . ." The servant who had been given one thousand coins then came in and said, "Sir. . .I was frightened and went out and hid your money in the ground. Here is every single coin!" The master of the servant told him, "You are lazy and good-for-nothing! You know that I harvest what I don't plant."*

MATTHEW 25:22–26 CEV

## Fresh Eyes of Faith

Relationships grow and change. If you're in a marriage relationship, recall that honeymoon phase. Loving each other seemed easy and exciting, pretty much all the time. Then comes everyday life. Apathy creeps in. The happiness you first felt may seem to fade. The same thing can happen with God. Don't settle for apathy when there's always more to love and discover about God. (And people!) Ask God to help you look at those you love, including Him, with fresh eyes.

## DAY 355

# Keep Going

Great faith is not the faith that walks always in the light and knows no darkness, but the faith that perseveres in spite of God's seeming silences.

FATHER ANDREW

Fold the arms of your faith and wait in quietness until the light goes up in your darkness. Fold the arms of your faith, I say, but not of your action. Think of something you ought to do, and go do it. Heed not your feelings. Do your work.

GEORGE MACDONALD

## DAY 356

# Grace Alone

It's humbling to accept a favor from someone, especially when you know it's one you can never repay. But that's what grace is: a gift so big you don't deserve it and can never repay it. All God asks is a tiny, mustard seed–sized grain of faith in return. When you tell God, "I believe," His grace wipes away everything that once came between you and Him. Lies. Anger. Betrayal. Pride. Selfishness. They're history, by God's grace alone.

DAY 357

*By Faith*

*That is why I am so eager to preach the
gospel also to you who are in Rome. For I
am not ashamed of the gospel, because it is
the power of God that brings salvation
to everyone who believes: first to the Jew,
then to the Gentile. For in the gospel
the righteousness of God is revealed—
a righteousness that is by faith from
first to last, just as it is written:
"The righteous will live by faith."*

ROMANS 1:15–17 NIV

## DAY 358

*Give the Utmost*

Consider what it would be like to own everything. Absolutely everything. Even the universe is under your control. It seems like it would be easy to be generous. After all, you've got so much. But God treasures every speck of His creation—especially His children. Entrusting us with free will, and with the job of caring for this planet, was a risky venture. Honor God's generosity by treating His gifts with the utmost love and care.

# DAY 359

## Heavenly Hope

Faith gives us many reasons for hope. A home in heaven is just one of them. But what exactly are you hoping for? The Bible tells us we'll receive a new body, one that never grows ill or old. Tears will be a thing of the past. We'll be in the company of angels, other believers, and God Himself. Scripture tells us words cannot fully describe what we'll find there. That's a hope worth holding on to.

## DAY 360

# Mary's Song

And Mary said, My soul doth magnify the Lord, and my spirit hath rejoiced in God my Saviour. For he hath regarded the low estate of his handmaiden: for, behold, from henceforth all generations shall call me blessed. For he that is mighty hath done to me great things; and holy is his name. And his mercy is on them that fear him from generation to generation.

LUKE 1:46–50 KJV

# Benevolent Balance

God is both merciful and just. His justice demands that restitution be made for the wrongs we've done. His mercy allows those wrongs to be paid for in full when we put our faith in Jesus' death and resurrection. One way of thanking God for this benevolent balance is by treating others fairly, mercifully, and with humility. When we "do the right thing" we love others the "right" way—a way that reflects our heavenly Father's own character.

## DAY 362

## Brain Power

Your brain is an amazing, God-given gift. It enables you to master new skills, solve complex problems, and mature in your understanding of life. In short, it enables you to learn. By reading the Bible, you learn how to grow in your faith. As you read, ask yourself, "What does this teach me about loving God and/or others?" Then apply what you learn to your daily life. Your brain, empowered by prayer, will teach you how.

DAY 363

*Not in Vain*

But by the grace of God I am what I am:
and his grace which was bestowed upon
me was not in vain; but I laboured
more abundantly than they all: yet not I,
but the grace of God which was with me.
Therefore whether it were I or they, so we
preach, and so ye believed. Now. . .how say
some among you that there is no resurrection
of the dead? . . . If Christ be not risen, then is
our preaching vain, and your faith is also vain.

1 CORINTHIANS 15:10–12, 14 KJV

## Shelter from the Storm

Your pumps are caked in mud. Your hair clings like a damp rag and you smell a bit like a wet schnauzer. But the rain doesn't let up. All you want is a warm, dry spot—a shelter from the storm. The Bible says you'll face all kinds of storms in this life. But God's your safe place, regardless of what's raging all around you. He's with you in every storm, offering protection and peace. Don't hesitate to draw near.

## DAY 365

## Secure in Faith

You can feel secure in your relationship with God. God doesn't suffer from mood swings or bad hair days. He isn't swayed by popular opinion or influenced by what others have to say about you. God's love, His character, His gift of salvation, and every promise He's ever made to you stands firm, immovable. You can lean on Him in any and every circumstance, secure in the fact that He'll never let you down.

# The Beginning and End

You control the beginning and end of all
that lives. You have given me the present,
and You lay out my future before me.
Your Word tells me that You've numbered
my days. Nothing, and no one, can alter
Your plans for me. Thank You, Lord, for being
my Shepherd. Thank You for watching over
and protecting me as a shepherd does
his sheep. And like my future, my faith
is under Your sovereign care. I am
saved and secure in Your arms! Amen.

Scripture Index

## OLD TESTAMENT

## NEW TESTAMENT

# Daily Inspiration for a Woman's Spirit!

### Daily Encouragement: 3-Minute Devotions for Women

Got 3 minutes to spare? Here you'll find the spiritual pick-me-up you desire in *Daily Encouragement: 3-Minute Devotions for Women.* This delightful daily devotional packs a powerful dose of comfort, encouragement, and joy into just-right-sized readings for women of all ages.

Paperback / 978-1-64352-505-1 / $9.99

### 365 Prayers for a Woman of God

This daily devotional prayer book is a lovely reminder for you to bring any petition before your heavenly Father. And 365 just-right-sized prayers touch on topics that resonate with the hearts of women of all ages and stages. Topics include: Grace, Blessings, Joy, Serving, Contentment, Difficulties, Rest, Surrender, Trust, and more.

Paperback / 978-1-64352-406-1 / $9.99